ENDORSEMENTS FOR *ASTOUNDING PROMISE*

I have just finished reading this remarkable book in one sitting. I say "remarkable" since that is exactly what it is. As I reflect on my years of training at theological college—then many years of pastoring in various residential church situations—I only wish I had had this book then! The pages immerse us in the promises—the ways—and the character of the Lord Himself!

John Hutchinson has masterfully encapsulated the heartbeat of God in this book. He has drawn together the key components of the Old and New Testaments and immersed them in easy to understand doctrine and theology. He has provided the end-time church with an amazing blueprint plan of God's eternal plan for humanity right from Eden to the return of Christ. John has given us a lens through which to view and understand the relevance of Scripture in this day and age—and most of all provides us with a hunger for the Holy Spirit and a desire to be tenacious for the things of God in these days in which the former and latter rains are converging.

What a time to be alive! God, through John, has given us a masterpiece; but then John is one of the true spiritual grandfathers of the 21st century church. This book should be read by every Christian, young and old, enquiring or mature. It informs, it challenges, and it answers questions. It will change your life forever!

—Rev. Dr. Alistair P. Petrie
Partnership Ministries

John's third and final release in his *Astounding* series is a joy and privilege to read, not only because of its practical and powerful truths, but because of the way John shares his personal experiences. The promise and presence of the Holy Spirit is a reality in his life. It's as though he is having a personal conversation with the reader.

I heartily recommend this book, both to those young in the faith and as a refreshing encouragement to the whole body of Christ worldwide.

—Rev. Don L. Harbridge

The Holy Spirit is often the least understood person of the Trinity. As a result, many sincere Christians are living joyless, ineffective lives, and lack a sense of His presence and power in their everyday lives and ministries.

In *Astounding Promise*, John Hutchinson shows how you can access the power of the Holy Spirit to transform the way you think, live, and minister. A respected scholar of God's Word, John starts with Genesis and takes readers on a journey through the Scriptures to a clear understanding of the Holy Spirit's nature and role. *Astounding Promise* clearly explains the difference between the indwelling of the Spirit when we are born again, and the empowerment we receive when we are baptized in the Holy Spirit.

John candidly shares his before and after experiences as a missionary in India. Before being baptized in the Holy Spirit, he experienced frequent frustration in his ministry, despite zealous efforts. The baptism of the Holy Spirit profoundly transformed his relationship with God, his relationship with others, and his effectiveness in ministry.

I love this book! If you yearn to experience God's presence in a deeper way, or if you long for a greater release of the Holy Spirit's power in your everyday life and ministry, this book is for you.

—Judy Rushfeldt
Award-winning author, speaker,
and online magazine publisher

The prayer of the Lord that God gave to me for this must-read book, *Astounding Promise*: Now therefore let it please You to bless this book of Your servant, John Hutchinson, that it may continue before You forever; for You, O Lord God, have inspired it, and with Your blessing let this book of Your servant guide multitudes to receive the astounding promise for themselves. (2 Samuel 7:29)

—Pastor John L. Teibe

Astounding Promise testifies to the true, Biblical Person who is the Holy Spirit. This trilogy of books is relevant to all people, especially a young generation who will experience the Holy Spirit in a new way, never seen before. Get ready. Get equipped. Receive God's astounding promise!

—Greg Frost
Every Nation Campus Minister, Calgary

Discussing the Holy Spirit within the context of the New Covenant is a difficult topic to tackle, and one that often becomes entrenched in theoretical theology. Through *Astounding Promise*, John Hutchinson brings a lovely human element to his argument by openly discussing the challenges and questions he faced while maturing in his faith and being transformed by God's Spirit. In a way that feels effortless, he places abstract spiritual concepts into a practical context that demonstrates how the Father provides guidance and opportunities for growth on a daily basis. This book offered a great amount of encouragement to me, and I would recommend it to anyone who desires to know more about the heart of God.

—Melissa Goertzen
Librarian, Columbia University

ASTOUNDING PROMISE

God Restores to Us the Fullness of His Spirit

John G. Hutchinson

ASTOUNDING PROMISE: GOD RESTORES TO US
THE FULLNESS OF HIS SPIRIT
Copyright © 2015 by John G. Hutchinson

All Scripture quotations, unless otherwise indicated, are taken from the New King James Version®. Copyright © 1982 by Thomas Nelson. Used by permission. All rights reserved.

Scripture quotations marked (AMP) are taken from the Amplified Bible, Copyright © 1954, 1958, 1962, 1964, 1965, 1987 by The Lockman Foundation. Used by permission.

Printed in Canada

ISBN: 978-1-4866-0809-6

Word Alive Press
131 Cordite Road, Winnipeg, MB R3W 1S1
www.wordalivepress.ca

WORD ALIVE
—P R E S S—

FSC
www.fsc.org

MIX
Paper from
responsible sources
FSC® C016245

Library and Archives Canada Cataloguing in Publication

Hutchinson, John G., 1932-, author
      Astounding promise : God restores to us the fullness of his spirit
/ John G. Hutchinson.

Issued in print and electronic formats.
ISBN 978-1-4866-0809-6 (pbk.).--ISBN 978-1-4866-0810-2 (pdf).--
ISBN 978-1-4866-0811-9 (html).--ISBN 978-1-4866-0812-6 (epub)

      1. Holy Spirit. I. Title.

BT121.3.H88 2015   231'.3   C2014-908111-1
                                             C2014-908112-X

TABLE OF CONTENTS

DEDICATION

I dedicate this book to glorify and exalt
Our wonderful Heavenly Father,
And His immeasurable *Astounding Love*
To each one of us, His precious children.

I also dedicate this book to glorify and exalt
Our wonderful Savior, Jesus Christ,
And His great, loving *Astounding Sacrifice*
For our forgiveness, and gift of eternal life.

I also dedicate this book to glorify and exalt
The wonderful, powerful Holy Spirit of God,
Who is God's great *Astounding Promise*
To all who have received Jesus, God's Son.

And I also dedicate this book as a memorial
To my wonderful, precious wife, Reta,
Who was a loving and vivacious partner.
God used her to uniquely bless many people.

Acknowledgements

I wholeheartedly give my thanks and appreciation to those of my family and friends who have encouraged me to write this third book. Many of the suggestions they made were actually words from the Lord to guide me.

I especially want to thank Carol Schmidt, the sister-in-Christ who, in faith, wrote out a short prophecy from the Lord, and handed it to me. Very shortly after that, God double-confirmed that this was truly a word from Him.

I also give great gratitude and appreciation to my dear friend, Janice Pasay, who has given a tremendous amount of help in writing this third book. She had helped me very, very much in writing and editing my first two books. But her help and wisdom this time has had to be much greater than before.

Because of some medical conditions that have come upon me, I have become very tired, both physically and mentally. These have made me lean on and depend on the Lord much more than ever before. Many times, after crying out to the Lord for help, I sensed Him giving me the inspiration for what to write, but at other times I felt weak and uninspired. Janice has had to do a tremendous job of editing, correcting, rearranging, consolidating, improving, and adding clarity to the manuscript.

Janice, I am at a loss for words to adequately express to you all my appreciation and gratitude, for all that you have done, and for your patience. I pray that the Lord will reward you greatly.

I am also grateful to those of my family, friends, and colleagues who have taken the time to peruse and critique my manuscript. They have given me good and helpful suggestions. God bless you all!

INTRODUCTION

This book, *Astounding Promise*, is the third in a trilogy. A trilogy is a set of three books, each continuing on with the same general subject. This trilogy is about the Trinity (Tri-unity) of God; namely, God the Father, God the Son, and God the Holy Spirit.

My first book, *Astounding Love: Experience God's Immeasurable Father-Love for You*, is mainly about the Father's great, eternal, passionate love for all of us, His created children.

God had to lean on me quite hard to get me to write and finish the first book. But I finally obeyed, got it published, and sighed a great sigh of relief. Very soon after that, I received from a sister-in-Christ, Carol Schmidt, who had read my book, a short written word from God—a prophecy—which said that I was to write two more books, and each of them was to have the word "Astounding" in the title. In the next few days, this word from God was confirmed and double-confirmed by several believers who did not know of the prophecy I had been given. Thus I was sure this message was from God, and so I obeyed.

Very quickly, the Lord revealed to me what the next two books were to be about, and their titles were given to me by Him. But it was not until I was working on the third book that I realized it would be the third book of a trilogy. This must have been the Lord's plan all along. It certainly was not planned by me! So I give Him all the credit and praise.

My second book, *Astounding Sacrifice: The Most Crucial Event in All of Human History*, is mainly about Jesus, God's sinless Son, taking on Himself all the sin of the whole human race, sacrificing Himself on the cross, and thus atoning (paying the full penalty) for all our sins. That book also portrays the significance of Jesus' death, burial, resurrection, and ascension to heaven's highest throne.

This third book, *Astounding Promise: God Restores to Us the Fullness of His Spirit*, is about the great Holy Spirit of God, promised by God as part of the New Covenant. It is about how the Holy Spirit can now come *in*, dwell *in*, and *unite with* our human spirits, making us new creations in Christ Jesus. It is also about the Holy Spirit coming *upon* us, filling us to overflowing, and empowering us to be witnesses to the world, of Jesus and His great salvation.

Just before starting this third book, several of my family and friends told me that they felt that I should include some of my own experiences with the Holy Spirit. I sensed that this was from the Lord, even though I am normally reticent to do so. I sensed that the Lord wanted me to do this so that the book wouldn't be just *theoretical* theology, but also give a sense of how His astounding promise is very real, experiential, and practical for all His born-again children. I pray that as you read this book, God will *fill you to overflowing* with His Spirit, for His glory!

CHAPTER ONE

IN THE VERY BEGINNING

A stounding promise?
What promise?
And what is so astounding?

It is astounding that God promised to give His great, perfect Holy Spirit in fullness and in power to us fallen, sinful—but redeemed—humans!

This is even more astounding when we see how great and powerful, and how absolutely holy and pure, is God's Spirit. And it is doubly astounding that God has promised to give His Holy Spirit to us, His redeemed-yet-imperfect people, as a completely free gift, by His great, loving grace! Jesus called this *"the Promise of the Father"* (Acts 1:4–5).

MY FIRST ENCOUNTER WITH JESUS AND HIS SPIRIT

Let me tell you briefly how I received the Spirit of God into my heart, into my spirit.

I had godly Christian parents, for which I am very grateful. But just as all humans since Adam's disobedience have had a sinful nature, I also have a fallen, sinful human nature. When I was seven years old, my mother caught me stealing something out of her purse. Normally I would have gotten a spanking for this, but this time God guided my mom differently.

I Had Sinned

She sat me down on the sofa and explained to me that I had broken one of God's laws—*"You shall not steal"* (Exodus 20:15)—and that this was a sin against God. Then she told me that God loved me so much that He sent His Son Jesus to die on the cross to pay for all our sins so that we could be forgiven. She told me that if I confessed my sin to God and asked for His forgiveness, I could invite Jesus to forgive me of all my sin, and to come into my heart to live there and give me eternal life. She helped me to pray a simple prayer asking Him to do this for me.

I Was Forgiven

And Jesus did do this for me. He Himself said, *"Let the little children come to Me, and do not forbid them; for of such is the kingdom of God"* (Mark 10:14). In childlike faith I received Him, His forgiveness, and His eternal life. I did not feel great emotion, but I did have a sense of relief and peace that I am sure came from God. I still clearly remember the incident right to this day.

God's Spirit Came Into My Spirit!

Jesus came into my spirit by His Spirit and, to use an expression Jesus used, I was *"born again"* (John 3:3), meaning that I was born spiritually. His Spirit united with my spirit. I was now His spiritual child. I love the fact that God, in His great love and wisdom, made the gospel simple enough for little children to receive it—in childlike faith!

What I experienced is exactly what God had in mind when He created us: God's Spirit united with our spirit.

GOD'S GREATEST GIFT TO ADAM AND EVE—HIS SPIRIT

Let's go back to the very beginnings of the human race and take a look at this astounding gift that God gave to Adam and Eve when He created them.

In Genesis 1:26, God said to Himself, *"Let Us make man [humans] in Our image, according to Our likeness."* This was His way of saying, "Let Us make humans to be just like Us, Our own precious children."

> *So God created man [humans] in His own image; in the image of God He created him; male and female He created them.*
> —Genesis 1:27

As God is a triune God—Father, Son, and Holy Spirit—He created man also as a triune being—body, soul (mind and emotions), and spirit—in His own image and in His own likeness, as His own dear children.

> *And the LORD God formed man of the dust of the ground, and breathed into his nostrils the breath of life; and man became a living being [soul].*
> —Genesis 2:7

Now, the Hebrew word translated "breath" here also means "wind" or "spirit." So God breathed not just air into Adam's lungs, He also breathed His own Spirit into Adam's spirit, and Adam became a living *spiritual* being, as well as a physical being. This is truly astounding!

Let's stop right here and think about this. The great, eternal, almighty Creator of heaven and earth breathed *His own life*—His nature, character, and the very essence of His Being—into His first little children whom He had just created. They didn't have to work to deserve or earn it. This was their birthright. This was their great loving Heavenly Father giving *Himself* as a *gift* to His own dear children. This is *truly astounding*, and sets apart mankind from every other creature on earth.

THE FULLNESS OF HIS SPIRIT

Do you suppose God gave Adam just a tiny little bit of His Spirit? No, that would not be like God! Scripture is full of statements which describe God as an incredibly loving, generous, good Father:

Doubtless You are our Father... You, O LORD, are our Father; our Redeemer from Everlasting is Your name.
—Isaiah 63:16

And the LORD passed before him [Moses] and proclaimed, "The LORD, the LORD God, merciful [full of mercy] and gracious [full of grace], longsuffering [full of patience], and abounding in goodness and truth,

*keeping mercy for thousands, forgiving iniquity and
transgression and sin..."*
—Exodus 34:6-7

The love of God as our Father is described in detail in my
earlier book, *Astounding Love: Experience God's Immeasurable
Father-Love for You*. I recommend this to you.

I am absolutely certain that God gave *the fullness* of His
Spirit to Adam and *filled* Adam *to overflowing* with His Spirit as
much as a perfectly created, sinless human could contain. This
is what His astounding promise—the fullness and power of His
Holy Spirit—is for us now. We will discuss this much more fully
later in this book.

After creating Adam, God created Eve by taking a rib from
Adam's side, making Eve a partner for Adam (Genesis 2:21-23).
Even though God created Eve in a different way, I am sure He
also filled Eve to overflowing with His Holy Spirit. Scripture
states that God created *both* Adam and Eve in the image of God
(Genesis 1:27). So every man and woman is created to be *filled*
with God's wonderful Holy Spirit! It is our precious birthright
from our loving Heavenly Father.

Love, Free Will, and Choice

Then God took Adam and Eve and put them in the Garden of
Eden, which He had planted for them, to tend it and cultivate
it (Genesis 2:15). Scripture indicates that God would walk and
talk with Adam and Eve in the garden in the cool of the day
(Genesis 3:8).

I am confident that God had a wonderful, loving relationship and intimate fellowship with His children, and that they

enjoyed their relationship with God, and He with them. He would teach them how to cultivate the garden and tend it, and give them His wisdom and instructions about how they should live. He was their incredibly loving, wise, and intimate Daddy. I am sure they and God enjoyed each other greatly! All of this was possible because God's Spirit was in them, and their spirits were perfectly united with God. When our hearts and minds are aligned through love, relationship is a joyous experience.

God told Adam and Eve that they could eat freely from every tree in the garden, except one. He commanded them *not* to eat from the tree of the knowledge of good and evil. And He warned them that if they ate the fruit of that tree, they would surely die that same day (Genesis 2:16-17).

Now why would God put a tree like that in Eden? Wasn't Eden the perfect place? Heaven on earth? God must have had a very good reason for including that tree.

God Is Eternal, Immeasurable Love

One of the greatest statements in Scripture is "God is love."

> *He who does not love does not know God, for* God is love... *And we have known [experienced] and believed the love that God has for us.* God is love...
> —1 John 4:8, 16 (emphasis added)

Twice in this chapter of Scripture, the Spirit of God says that love is Who God is—not just what He has, nor what He gives, nor what He does, but *Who He is*—at the very center of His Being. So, love is the main characteristic of God's nature and the essence of His Being.

GOD GAVE MAN A FREE WILL

I am certain that the main reason God created humans as His own dear children is because He wanted to be in a *love* relationship with them—to love them greatly, and for them to love Him wholeheartedly in return. Love will crave to give love freely, but it will crave for love to be eagerly and *voluntarily* returned as well. It should be a two-way relationship. God made it that way. He gave Adam and Eve a free will so that they could *freely choose* to receive God's great love, and *freely choose* to eagerly love Him in return and *voluntarily* obey Him. But in order for love to be voluntary, there must be an alternative, a choice; otherwise we would be just like slaves or robots—with no choice! So God gave Adam and Eve a command which provided an alternative: choose to obey Him, or choose to disobey Him.

Knowing the difference between good and evil is one of the definitions of wisdom. "Good" means beneficial, and "evil" means detrimental and harmful; wisdom is knowing the difference between the two. I believe the reason God gave this command to Adam and Eve was so that *He alone* would be their source of wisdom and direction, and that they should *not* make decisions on their own, but seek Him for His wisdom. God was, and rightfully wanted to be, the Lord, the Master, the Shepherd, and the Father of mankind. He, and He *only*, has all knowledge and wisdom (1 Timothy 1:17), and He is the *only* One who has the right to guide our lives.

DECEPTION, DISOBEDIENCE, AND DEATH

But satan came along to tempt Adam and Eve to disobey God (Genesis 3:1-5). Satan was originally one of the highest angels in heaven, but he became proud and wanted to be equal to God. He led a rebellion of other angels, and became God's enemy (Isaiah 14:12-15; Ezekiel 28:14-18; Luke 10:18; Revelation 12:7-9). He hates God and all that God loves, especially God's people.

Satan came and first *questioned* what God said. He asked, "Are you sure God said that you shouldn't eat of every tree in the garden?" (see Genesis 3:1). Then he *contradicted* what God said: "No, you won't die" (see Genesis 3:4). Then he turned their attention on *themselves*, rather than on God: "God knows that when you eat the fruit, your understanding will be opened, and you will be like God, knowing both good and evil" (see Genesis 3:5). Thus satan tempted them by telling them that they would be *like* God (Genesis 3:5), inferring that they would be wise, able to control their own lives and make their own decisions. They were deceived by this, because they were never meant to be independent of God's guidance and control!

Self and self-exaltation, which is *pride*, and wanting to control our own lives, be independent, and make our own decisions *without God* is the very root of our fallen, sinful human nature ever since Adam sinned. We were *not* created to run our own lives and make our own decisions *without Him*!

Both Adam and Eve listened to satan and ate the forbidden fruit, disobeying God. Immediately they felt shame and tried to cover themselves, for they were naked. Their emotional and spiritual discomfort made them physically uncomfortable. So when they heard the voice of God calling them, they were afraid and hid themselves and covered themselves with fig leaves (Genesis 3:7-10).

GOD PROMISES SALVATION

The Lord made coats of the skins of animals, and used them to clothe Adam and Eve to cover their nakedness (Genesis 3:21). This necessitated the slaying of animals and shedding their blood. This is a prophetic picture of Jesus, who would shed His blood on the cross to pay the penalty for all our sins, and thus cover us with His perfect righteousness.

Then God told satan, *"[The Seed of the woman] shall bruise your head, and you shall bruise His heel"* (Genesis 3:15). This is another prophetic reference to Jesus and His future crucifixion. God, in His foreknowledge, already had salvation planned for the whole human race!

But it was Adam and Eve who were supposed to have died that day, not these animals. God had warned them that *"in the day that you eat of it [the tree of the knowledge of good and evil] you shall* surely *die"* (Genesis 2:17, emphasis added). Adam and Eve did not die *physically* on the day they ate the forbidden fruit. In fact, they lived for many years after (Genesis 5:5). Was God's Word not fulfilled?

GOD IS ETERNALLY, ABSOLUTELY HOLY

Yes, it was. Adam and Eve did die that day. As soon as they sinned by eating the forbidden fruit, they died *spiritually.* Even though their bodies and souls remained alive, *their spirits died.* Their spirits had become spiritually alive when God breathed His Spirit into them. But when they sinned, the Spirit of God withdrew from within them, because God is absolutely holy. He could *not* remain in unity and harmony with them. That would violate His holy, sinless nature.

What does the word "holy" mean? In both the Old Testament and the New Testament, we see that the angels in heaven are crying out continually, "Holy, holy, holy is the Lord God Almighty!" (see Isaiah 6:3; Revelation 4:8). Repeating "holy" three times indicates strong emphasis.

I have thoroughly studied the root meanings of the word "holy" in the English, Hebrew, and Greek languages, and have come up with this definition: holiness means "total perfection and perfect totality." God is whole, entire, complete, pure, undefiled, undiminished, undiluted, absolute perfection. He is one complete harmonious whole—perfectly integrated, perfectly balanced, perfectly complete—all the time, forever. The holiness of God embraces His entire Being—everything He is. Every aspect of His attributes, strengths, abilities, character traits, thoughts, actions, and emotions is total perfection and perfect totality.

God loves truth, and He hates untruth. God loves faithfulness, and He hates unfaithfulness. God loves righteousness, and He hates unrighteousness. God loves justice, and He hates injustice. This is His completely holy nature (Hebrews 1:8-9). God said to Jesus, when He brought Him into the world, "*You have loved righteousness and hated lawlessness; therefore God, Your God, has anointed You with the oil of gladness more than Your companions*" (Hebrews 1:9).

AN ILLUSTRATION

An illustration of this is a good, totally-loving human father who passionately wants the highest and best for his precious little children. Because of his great love for them, he will hate everything that would in any way rob, hurt, pervert, or destroy his precious children. Jesus said,

The thief [satan] does not come except to steal, and to kill, and to destroy. I have come that they may have life, and that they may have it more abundantly. I am the good shepherd. The good shepherd gives His life for the sheep.

—John 10:10-11

THE IMMENSE TRAGEDY!

The holy God cannot be in partnership or in any union with sin. So He had to remove Himself from Adam's and Eve's spirits. This was an immense tragedy! Their spirits, which were made to be *filled* with the Holy Spirit of the Living God, immediately became dead, empty, ashamed, and lonely, even though their bodies and souls remained alive.

From then on, until God eventually manifested Himself to the world by Jesus Christ and sacrificed Him on the cross for the payment of all our sins, the human spirit could *not* have this same marvelous fullness, oneness, and deep intimacy with the Holy Spirit of God, as Adam and Eve had before they sinned.

BUT JESUS HAS COME

Now that Jesus has come, and has paid for all the sins of the whole human race on that cruel, cruel cross, and is risen from the dead, triumphant and victorious, we can be forgiven and completely washed *"whiter than snow"* (Psalms 51:7) by His shed blood! When we receive Christ, we also receive the Holy Spirit of God back into our human spirits and become spiritually alive again, united with God. We will talk more about this later.

AND YOU, TOO, CAN RECEIVE JESUS AND HIS SPIRIT

I urge you with all my heart to humble yourself before God, confess your sinfulness, repent (turn back to God), ask for forgiveness, and receive the Person of the crucified, resurrected, and ascended Christ. Receive all that He did for you on that cross on Calvary. *Receive* Jesus as your Savior and your Lord, in childlike faith, even if you're a complicated, sophisticated, intellectual adult. And *give* yourself to Him.

Jesus says, *"Behold, I stand at the door and knock. If anyone hears My voice and opens the door, I will come in to him and dine [feast] with him, and he with Me"* (Revelation 3:20). He will not force Himself upon you. Ask Him, invite Him, to come into your life as your Lord, and give yourself to Him. He has promised to come in to you by His Spirit! You will be completely forgiven and have the gift of eternal life—all by His free and abundant grace! You can have God's Spirit unite with your spirit, and begin to make you a new person, right now, if you will take that step—in sincere childlike faith!

> *Let us therefore come boldly to the throne of grace, that we may obtain mercy and find grace to help in time of need.*
>
> —Hebrews 4:16

> *For by grace you have been saved through faith, and that not of yourselves; it is the gift of God, not of works, lest anyone should boast.*
>
> —Ephesians 2:8–9

CHAPTER TWO

FROM ADAM'S FALL
TO CHRIST'S REDEMPTION

WHAT ADAM AND EVE LOST

When Adam and Eve disobeyed God and sinned against Him, they suffered a terrible loss. One time, God gave me a deep revelation of the difference between what Adam and Eve had before their fall—what God originally intended for all people—and what Adam and Eve, and all of us, lost in the fall. Believe it or not, God gave me this revelation in a movie theater!

About two years after my wife Reta and I were filled with the Holy Spirit in Bombay, India, we returned to Canada. Some Spirit-filled friends of ours told us of a wonderful movie they had just seen. They strongly urged us to go and see it, so we went. The movie was *Fiddler on the Roof*.

Now, it is a good classic movie, but near the end of it God gave me a very deep and overwhelming revelation of two realities far beyond anything the movie itself could have given, or that I could have imagined on my own. It is still, to this day, beyond my power to adequately describe. I just don't have the words!

First, God showed me what He, in His great love, original-ly intended for all of us to experience and enjoy on earth: the complete love, relationship, harmony, unity, peace, contentment, happiness, joy, delight, pleasure, fulfillment, goodness, kindness, tenderness, health, purpose, destiny, righteousness, and continual, sweet, loving communion with Him—if we had *not* fallen into sin.

This astounding revelation opened my eyes to the wonderful and indescribable love and goodness of God's heart for every one of us whom He created, and whom He loves so intensely. This revelation greatly astounded me, and transformed and deepened my personal love for God—and it still continues to do so!

But then God imposed upon this superbly glorious reality something horribly opposite to it. God showed me the depth and ugly reality of what sin and satan have done to the human race, in stark contrast to the great love and goodness God intended for us. It is also beyond my power to adequately describe what I saw: the pain, brokenness, suffering, sorrow, agony, misery, enmity, anger, bitterness, unforgiveness, malice, hatred, murder, sickness, death, fear, rejection, greed, poverty, brutality, abuse, injustice, war, and genocide.

This horrible second revelation opened my eyes to the vindictiveness, vicious hatred, murderous maliciousness, and vile destructiveness of satan's nature and character. This horrible second realization of what satan is still inflicting on us highlighted all the more, by extreme contrast, the glorious true love and goodness of God's wonderful heart toward us, which is a side of God few people seem to know and experience.

These totally opposite revelations, so vividly superimposed against each other, were almost more than I could bear. I was overwhelmed! I began to sob from the deepest part of my being. But since I was in a crowded theater, I had to sob silently. My wife could not imagine what was happening to me, because

I had never been so emotional before. We were the last ones to leave the theater, and I couldn't compose myself enough to tell her about it until we were more than halfway home.

This revelation made it clear to me what Adam and Eve lost when they disobeyed God. God's Holy Spirit had to depart from their now-sinful spirits, leaving their spirits dead, empty, and lonely. They still had a spirit, but they could not commune with God or be filled with His Spirit as God originally intended.

But God Still Loved Them!

But Adam and Eve were still God's precious children! He still passionately loved them and fervently desired intimacy with them. Their cold, dead, empty spirits were an encouragement— actually a gift—from God to make them realize their need for the Spirit to dwell within them.

Remember that God is eternal love. This is His very heart and nature. He is full of mercy, grace, compassion, patience, and forgiveness (Exodus 34:6-7). He still loved His children, even though their sin grieved Him and broke His heart. God could *not* be in the same union with them and as intimate with them as He had been before. *But* He continued to love them.

Even though there were many awful consequences of Adam's and Eve's sin, all of which were passed on to the rest of the human race, God did *not* forsake them. He would still talk to them and try to lead and guide them.

As we have seen, God immediately prophesied that the Seed of Eve, who is Jesus Christ, would crush satan's head (Genesis 3:15). God also clothed Adam and Eve with the skins of slain animals, which was a prophetic picture of Jesus being slain for our sins, forgiving us and covering us with His perfect righteousness.

> *Therefore, just as through one man sin entered the world, and death through sin, and thus death spread to all men, because all sinned... For as by one man's disobedience many were made sinners, so also by one Man's obedience many will be made righteous... so that as sin reigned in death, even so grace might reign through righteousness to eternal life through Jesus Christ our Lord.*
>
> —Romans 5:12, 19, 21

MY EXPERIENCE OF GOD PROTECTING AND FORGIVING

I have told you the story of how I received Jesus Christ into my heart, into my spirit, when I was seven years old. There is no doubt in my mind that at that time, I was "born" spiritually by the Spirit of God (John 3:3), and that He dwelt within me in my spirit. But when I got into my early teenage years, I began to drift away from the Lord, getting involved with the wrong crowd and intensely desiring to experience lustful sins.

In spite of having opportunities to fulfill these desires, for some reason I did not take them. At the time, I could not understand what stopped me, and was very frustrated. Later on, I realized that the Spirit of God within me was protecting me. I am sure that my parents were praying very much for me during this time.

I can remember coming home one night after being out with the wrong crowd. I got into bed but was unable to fall asleep. I was troubled and felt guilty. I felt confused and convicted of sin. The Holy Spirit was strongly speaking to me! For a long time I struggled, but finally I got out of my bed, knelt in the dark, and said, "Oh God, I don't know whether or not I'm still saved. If I am lost, please save me right now. If I am still saved, then get me out of this mess and turn me around. I ask You in Jesus' name."

I am sure that I was still saved, and God did get me out of that mess. He began to turn me around, and eventually brought me to the point where I fully dedicated my life to Jesus Christ and to His Lordship. He enabled me to live and witness for Him in my high school years, and then go on to graduate from Bible college. Even when I had not been seeking God, He pursued me and brought me back into relationship with Himself.

Throughout Human History, God Continues to Love, Guide, and Forgive

Despite the sins of His children, starting with Adam and Eve and throughout the ages, God still loved them, and He continued to bless them, guide them, and speak to them. He was even eager to forgive them!

God Blessed His People

All the way through Old Testament history, story after story tells us how God walked with, communed with, blessed, guided, provided for, and protected His people, His precious children. To mention just a few, there are the stories of Enoch, Noah, Job, Abraham, Isaac, Jacob/Israel, and Joseph.

- Enoch *"walked with God"* and was taken to be with God (Genesis 5:24).
- Noah *"found grace in the eyes of the LORD"* (Genesis 6:8), so God saved Noah and his family from the flood that covered all the earth (Genesis 6-8).

- Although God allowed Job to be severely tested (Job 1:6-19), in the end, He *"blessed the latter days of Job more than his beginning"* (Job 42:12).
- God led childless Abraham out of his country, but promised him a new land and innumerable descendants (Genesis 12:1-3, 13:14-17, 15:1-5).
- God spared Isaac and provided Abraham with a ram in his place as an offering to God, confirming His promise to multiply Abraham's descendants and bless all nations with them (Genesis 22:1-18).
- God prospered Jacob even when his father-in-law tried to cheat him (Genesis 31:1-13).
- Although Joseph's brothers sold him as a slave, God protected him and used him to save his family and all of Egypt from starvation in a famine (Genesis 37-47).

Throughout the generations, the Spirit of God was working greatly with and through His people, in love and mercy, patience, and forgiveness.

God Spoke to His People

There are also accounts of how God used Moses to deliver the children of Israel from four hundred years of slavery in Egypt, and how God led them through the wilderness, provided for them miraculously, gave them His laws, and finally led them into the promised land for their inheritance (Exodus 3-40; Numbers 1-36). There are the stories of Joshua, Samuel, King David, King Solomon, and the many prophets, through whom the Spirit of God spoke, teaching, encouraging, reproving, rebuking, chastening, and warning His people.

- Led by God, Joshua led the Israelites into the land promised to them by God (Joshua 1-11).

- God used Samuel to warn the Israelites against wanting a king to rule over them (1 Samuel 8:1-22), but then directed him to anoint Saul as king of Israel when the people chose to have a king rather than God to rule over them (1 Samuel 8:19-22, 10:17-25, 16:1-13).

- David wrote many of the Psalms, which describe God and encourage worship of God (for example, Psalm 103).

- Solomon wrote much of the book of Proverbs, which teaches right behavior and warns against immorality (for example, Proverbs 28:12).

- Isaiah, Jeremiah, Ezekiel, Hosea, Micah, and many other prophets warned about judgment falling on those who turned away from God (for example, Isaiah 65:1-7; Jeremiah 11:1-17; Hosea 4:1-10).

Thus God, through His Holy Spirit, lovingly fathered and shepherded His dear created children, especially His chosen people, Israel.

God Gave the Scriptures to His People

From Moses until the time of Christ, the Spirit of God spoke to, and through, many of His people, and had them write down the words He gave them. This is the way that the Spirit of God recorded the written Word of God—the Old Testament Scripture—which has been preserved by God to speak to all the rest of human history.

*All Scripture is given by inspiration of God, and is
profitable for doctrine, for reproof, for correction, for
instruction in righteousness, that the man [or woman]
of God may be complete, thoroughly equipped for every
good work.*

—2 Timothy 3:16-17

*And so we have the prophetic word confirmed... know-
ing this first, that no prophecy of Scripture is of any pri-
vate interpretation, for prophecy never came by the will
of man, but holy men of God spoke as they were moved
by the Holy Spirit.*

—2 Peter 1:19-21

GOD PROVIDED A WAY OF FORGIVENESS

So throughout this long period of time—from Adam to Christ—
we see that God's Holy Spirit was still very loving and active in
the lives of people.

But God was still external. Even though He spoke to and led
His people and gave them His Word in written form, it was external to them. It was merely a small taste of what God intended
to give mankind, in the future, through Christ. God could not
dwell *within* them as He had lived within and filled Adam and
Eve, or commune with them as He had communed with them,
before they sinned.

Because of God's great love for people and His desire for
intimate relationship with them, He provided a way for the sins
of His people to be covered until Jesus came. God instituted a
requirement: that people should offer to Him animal sacrifices,
the shedding of innocent blood, for the forgiveness (covering)

of their sins, until Jesus came to die for the sins of all human history. (The events of Jesus' death and resurrection and what they mean for us are described in detail in my second book, *Astounding Sacrifice: The Most Crucial Event in All of Human History*.)

From the time of Adam and Eve's fall throughout the Old Testament period, God revealed this requirement of blood sacrifice to each generation. Godly men and women expressed their repentance and faith by offering blood sacrifices to God, believing their sins would be forgiven (covered).

The concept of blood sacrifices is originally seen in the lives of the first two children born to Adam and Eve. Cain, the firstborn, offered to the Lord vegetables, the fruit of the ground, which did not involve a blood sacrifice. Abel, his younger brother, offered to the Lord the firstlings of his flock of sheep, which did involve a blood sacrifice. God was *not* pleased with Cain's offering and rejected it, but He was *well-pleased* with Abel's sacrifice and accepted it. So Cain murdered his brother! (Genesis 4:2–8)

But this system of sacrifice did not restore the same relationship between God and people that Adam and Eve first enjoyed. It was only a temporary measure.

For it is not possible that the blood of bulls and goats could take away sins.
—Hebrews 10:4

But Christ came as High Priest of the good things to come, with the greater and more perfect tabernacle [temple] not made with hands, that is, not of this creation. Not with the blood of goats and calves, but with His own blood He entered the Most Holy Place [in heaven] once for all, having obtained eternal redemption. For if the blood of bulls and goats and the ashes of a heifer, sprinkling the unclean, sanctifies for the purifying of the flesh, how much more *shall the blood of Christ, who through the eternal Spirit offered Himself without spot to God, cleanse your conscience from dead works to serve the living God?*

—Hebrews 9:11-14 (emphasis added)

CHAPTER THREE

GOD PROMISES A NEW COVENANT

THE NEW COVENANT ILLUSTRATED

Shortly after I graduated from Bible college, I married a fellow student, a wonderful, vivacious, Christ-loving gal named Reta, and we accepted an invitation to pastor a little church in a small town in southern Alberta, Canada. However, Reta and I had already clearly heard the Lord telling us that He wanted us to become missionaries in a foreign country. Taking on the little church was to gain experience as we waited on God for further direction.

During the second year of us pastoring this little church, a family that was going to India as missionaries asked if they could speak to our church and present their proposed work, and ask for prayer and financial support. We agreed. So they came and told our congregation that they would be working in Bombay with high school and university students, the future leaders of the next generation, under the organization Youth for Christ International. This was startling to us, because we had a preconceived idea that missionaries went to small villages and ministered to poor people. What they described was very appealing to us, because we had already been quite active and successful in working with high school students.

I couldn't get this out of my mind for several days, and I began to sense this might be God calling us to do this kind of ministry in India. But I was afraid Reta might not feel this way, so I decided to share this with her the next day at lunch. I began to tell her, and to my surprise she began to tell me she was feeling the same way, and had also been afraid to talk to me about it. In fact, she had decided the day before that she would share this with me at this same lunchtime. Immediately we saw that God was leading and guiding us both to this ministry.

God wonderfully provided, confirming His leading to us, and in about a year and a half we and our two very young daughters arrived in India for a five-year term.

It was in India that God fully immersed me in His Spirit. More about this later.

FROM OLD TO NEW

What Reta and I experienced is an example of God's desire for each one of us: that His Spirit lives in us and communes with us. This is the promise of the New Covenant. The New Covenant was instituted by Jesus. Until then, the Old Covenant prevailed. Let's look at both covenants more closely.

THE OLD COVENANT

During the long period between Adam's fall and the crucifixion of Christ, there was a time when God's chosen people, Israel, were in slavery in Egypt for four hundred years. God raised up Moses, one of the greatest leaders in Old Testament history, to lead Israel out of bondage in Egypt and through the wilderness of Mount Sinai, on their way to the land God had promised to give them (Exodus 1:1-19:2).

At Mount Sinai, God spoke the Ten Commandments to Israel, in a thundering voice that shook the ground and terrified both the people and Moses (Exodus 19:9-20). Later, God gave Moses the Ten Commandments engraved on tablets of stone (Exodus 32:15-16; 34:1-4).

At that time, God made a covenant with Moses and the people of Israel: if they would obey God and continue to keep these Ten Commandments, He would bless them and make them His special, holy nation (Exodus 34:10-28). God also established a very detailed system of blood sacrifices to offer to Him for the forgiveness of their sins (Exodus 24:3-8). This provision for the forgiveness (covering) of their sins is a manifestation of the great love, mercy, and grace of God. It shows again how much He desires relationship with us.

God had Moses write the first five books of the Old Testament (Covenant), which included human history up to that point, a description of the holy tabernacle (tent), and the details of many other laws, ordinances, rituals, and special holy feast days. The covenant of the Ten Commandments and all other laws, ordinances, and rituals is referred to in Scripture as *"the law of God"* (Romans 7:22), *"the law of the LORD"* (Psalm 119:1), *"the law of Moses"* (1 Corinthians 9:9), or just *"the law"* (Romans 8:3-4). "The law" was in force during the period of time that lasted from Moses until the crucifixion of Jesus Christ (Galatians 3:19, 23-25).

THE PROBLEM WAS...

The Old Covenant made a way for God's people to receive forgiveness, through the blood sacrifices, and gave them guidance in how to approach God. However, God's Spirit remained separate from them. The problem was that while they received forgiveness for their sins, the Old Covenant did not give them the power to stop sinning. The law left God's Spirit outside of them, so they continued to sin and had to make offerings to God again and again without it changing their sinful nature.

> *For if that first covenant had been faultless, then no place would have been sought for a second.*
> —Hebrews 8:7 (see also verses 8-13)

The blood sacrifices were just a picture of Christ's future death and resurrection, in which He would provide forgiveness for sins once and for all. Christ's one sacrifice provided complete forgiveness for all of human history, and never had to be repeated.

> *For by one offering He [Jesus] has perfected forever those who are being sanctified [made holy].*
> —Hebrews 10:14 (see also verses 1-17)

GOD PROMISES TO PUT HIS SPIRIT WITHIN US

What God truly desired was the relationship He had enjoyed with Adam and Eve in the Garden of Eden, when His Spirit lived *within* them. Although God instituted the Old Covenant for a period of time, it was not everything He intended to give. So from the time of Adam until the arrival of Christ, God spoke through many prophets, psalmists, and others who wrote what they heard from God, promising to restore what He originally provided. These writings are included in the Old Testament Scriptures, which God has preserved to this day.

Through two of these prophets, Jeremiah and Ezekiel (who lived about 590 years before Jesus was born), God foretold of a time when He would make a *New* Covenant to replace the Old Covenant—the law. Let's take a look at these great promises of a New Covenant.

The New Covenant Prophesied

Through the prophet Jeremiah, God said that He would make a new covenant that would *not* be according to the covenant He made through Moses:

> *Behold, the days are coming, says the* LORD, *when I will make a* new *covenant with the house of Israel and with the house of Judah—not according to the covenant that I made with their [forefathers] in the day that I took them by the hand to lead them out of the land of Egypt, My covenant which they broke, though I was a husband to them, says the* LORD. *But this is the covenant that I will make with the house of Israel after those days, says the* LORD: *I will put My law* in their minds, *and write it* on their hearts; *and I will be their God, and they shall be My people. No more shall every man teach his neighbor, and every man his brother, saying, "Know the* LORD," *for they all shall know Me, from the least of them to the greatest of them, says the* LORD. *For I will forgive their iniquity, and their sin I will remember no more.*
> —Jeremiah 31:31-34 (emphasis added)

Notice that God said, "I will put My law *in* their minds, and write it *on* their hearts." He also said, "I will forgive their iniquity, and their sin I will remember no more." This really is wonderfully new and astounding! This is far beyond what the Old Covenant could do. In the Old Covenant, God's laws were written on tablets of stone, and later on leather scrolls, and God was instructing people to keep His commandments (Exodus 19:5). The Old Covenant was outside of them, *not* within them.

A New Heart and a New Spirit Within

Now let's look at what God said through the prophet Ezekiel. This is almost identical to what God said through Jeremiah, but gives more light on God's promised New Covenant.

> *Then I will sprinkle clean water on you, and you shall be clean; I will cleanse you from all your filthiness and from all your idols. I will give you a* new *heart and put a* new *spirit within you; I will take the [hard] heart of stone out of your flesh and give you a [tender] heart of flesh. I will put* My Spirit *within you and* cause you *to walk in My statutes, and you will* keep *My judgments and* do *them.*
> —Ezekiel 36:25-27 (emphasis added)

Here God says that not only will He give us a *new* heart and put a *new* spirit within us, He promises to put *His Spirit* within us and cause (enable, empower) us to walk in His statutes, so that we will be able to keep His commandments and do them. Thus, the apostle Paul writes in the New Testament:

> *Do you not know that you are the temple of God and that the Spirit of God dwells* in *you?*
> —1 Corinthians 3:16 (emphasis added)

*Or do you not know that your body is the temple of the
Holy Spirit who is in you, whom you have from God,
and you are not your own?*
—1 Corinthians 6:19 (emphasis added)

This is God beginning to give back to us what we lost when
Adam sinned. God's precious Holy Spirit can now dwell *within* us,
because the New Covenant that Jesus purchased for us through
His crucifixion and resurrection has now blotted out *all* our sin
and iniquity. The holy, holy Holy Spirit of God can now *unite*
with, be one with, and be intimate with our cleansed and completely forgiven human spirits. This is astoundingly good news!

Now, in the New Covenant we have in Christ, God by His
Spirit *within* us enables us and gives us the power to obey Him
and walk in His ways. This is far beyond what the Old Covenant—the law—could ever do for us! The New Covenant is God
within us, making us *new*, and empowering us to *obey* Him, with
His power, *not* our own.

*[F]or it is God who works in you both to will and to do
for His good pleasure.*
—Philippians 2:13 (emphasis added)

GOD'S SPIRIT AT WORK IN ME

My Own Zealous Striving and Hard Work Resulted in Failure

Our first term in southern India with Youth for Christ was fairly
fruitful. We had to learn a lot about the people and their cus-
toms. However, we were able to lead a good number of people
to Christ, especially one college student who had great potential

for leadership. Several years later, after some discipleship and training, he went on to become an outstanding Christian leader in the large city of Calcutta (later renamed Kolkata).

Our two sons were born in India during this first term. After our term was completed, we came home to Canada for a one-year furlough to give us some rest and to raise more prayer support and financial support. Reta and I knew that God wanted us to return to India for another five-year term. During the furlough, I took more training and got some more experience in directing a Youth for Christ rally.

Upon returning, we were assigned to Bombay (later renamed Mumbai). I returned to India full of self-confidence, having received more training and experience. I was full of zeal and enthusiasm, determined to make Bombay Youth for Christ a great success. I began to zealously strive and work very hard, trying my best to think of ways to attract the young people to our meetings.

However, after a while I noticed that both the attendance and finances were going down. This made me try even more zealously and work harder. But the harder I tried, the farther down it went. It began to wear me out.

Then, one day as I was driving alone in my car to the office, I said out loud to God, "God, if You can do anything with this work of Yours, then go ahead and do it. But I quit trying to make it go. I have tried my very best and it's still going downhill. I will just do what needs to get done, but I cannot push anymore."

I Quit Trying Hard

To my astonishment, I heard clearly in my spirit God say a loud, "Good." I was shocked! I was also puzzled, thinking to myself, *What kind of a God is this?* But I did quit pushing and trying. In fact, I was actually trapped, because we didn't have the money to go back to Canada. So I just did the basic things that needed doing.

After a couple of months, I began to realize that the attendance and finances were increasing, and that good things were happening. So I said to God, "It's not fair. I just about burn myself out, and it goes down. But when I quit trying hard, it goes up." And again, I clearly heard God say, "Good." This time I got angry. I was greatly perplexed. And I found myself going downhill spiritually.

About this time, the pastor of Bombay Baptist Church asked me if, in addition to my Youth for Christ work, I would handle the Sunday services for one year as interim pastor. He was going back to England on furlough and they had no one to replace him. He said that if we accepted the position, we could stay in the living quarters above the church, free of charge. I wasn't really interested, because I was aware of some problems the church was facing. But to be polite, I said I would pray about it. In order to be honest, I did pray about it. And I was very surprised when I heard God say, "Take it." So we did.

But I was continuing to become spiritually dry and empty. I could not get much insight, comfort, or direction from reading my Bible. I could hardly pray. And I was having difficulty thinking of sermons to preach. At the time, I did not realize what was happening. The truth only came to me a while later.

A Very Wrong Belief

In my Bible college years, I memorized John 15:5, where Jesus says, *"I am the vine, you are the branches. He who abides in*

Me, and I in him, bears much fruit; for without Me you can do nothing."

Although I had memorized the verse, I had loosely and very wrongly translated its meaning. Jesus said that *"without [Him] you can do* nothing" (emphasis added). Nothing means nothing. Zero. I had wrongly thought we were to do all we could in our own power, in our own wisdom, with our own efforts, and then be humble enough to admit that we need Him to help us a little bit. How wrong I was!

Yes, I had the Holy Spirit of Jesus in me, and I was sincere in serving Him. And I was very zealous. But I was *not* relying on Him, *nor* trusting in Him, *nor* calling upon Him to work through me in *His* power. I realized later that God was bringing me down to zero, so that I would depend on *His* wisdom and *His* power, for *His* glory, *not* for mine. I also realized later that He was breaking the pride that I didn't know I had!

Chapter Four

God's Promise of the
New Covenant Is Fulfilled

We have seen how the promise of a New Covenant was given. But how would the New Covenant be instituted? By what means would God seal the New Covenant between Himself and His people? As with every other aspect of our relationship with God, God takes the initiative Himself.

The Holy Spirit Alone Works
the New Covenant in Us

It is important to realize that God alone can change our hearts and conform us to the image of Christ. He spoke this to me very clearly one time when I was meditating on the fruit of the Spirit: love, joy, peace, longsuffering, kindness, goodness, faithfulness, gentleness, and self-control (Galatians 5:22-23).

As I went through the list, I said to myself that the Holy Spirit must grow and develop all these things in me. But when I came to the last one, self-control, I said to myself that I must develop much more self-control. And immediately I heard God say, "No, you cannot control your old self. That is the work of the Holy Spirit. He is the *only One* who can conquer and control your old sinful self. Trust the Holy Spirit to develop this, and do *not* trust your own efforts!"

THE MESSIAH IS PROMISED

God promised that satan's head would be crushed by the Seed of the woman, a Savior or Messiah Who would bring liberty from the bondage that resulted from the fall of Adam and Eve. The Hebrew word "Messiah" means the One sent from God, consecrated for a special purpose by anointing with special oil. The Greek word for Messiah is "Christ."

During the long period of "the law" (from Moses until Christ), many prophecies were given through the psalmists and prophets about the coming Messiah, including His miraculous birth, and especially many details about His betrayal, death, and resurrection. The Old Testament is filled with prophecies about the Messiah.

God prophesied Messiah's miraculous birth in this way:

Therefore the Lord Himself will give you a sign: Behold, the virgin shall conceive and bear a Son, and shall call His name Immanuel [which means "God with us"].
—Isaiah 7:14

For unto us a Child is born, unto us a Son is given; and the government will be upon His shoulder. And His name will be called Wonderful, Counselor, Mighty God, Everlasting Father, Prince of Peace.
—Isaiah 9:6

For several hundred years, the Jews were looking, eagerly longing, and praying for their promised Messiah to come, set up His kingdom, and set them free. The Jewish people believed that the Messiah would save the nation of Israel from foreign military domination and become their glorious King. However, as we saw earlier, God had something else in mind: an internal heart change rather than an external political change. God's concern is always with our hearts and our relationship with Him. Thus, the Messiah sent by God would save the Jewish people from their sins, rather than saving them from the Romans who occupied their land.

THE MESSIAH IS GIVEN

And in God's perfect time, the Messiah came. The angel Gabriel was sent by God to the virgin Mary to announce His coming (Luke 1:26–38). The angel said,

> *And behold, you will conceive in your womb and bring forth a Son, and shall call His name JESUS [which means "God saves"]... The Holy Spirit will come upon you, and the power of the Highest will overshadow you; therefore, also, that Holy One who is to be born will be called the Son of God.*
>
> —Luke 1:31, 35

The conception of Jesus was a great miracle of God: Mary conceived by the power of the Holy Spirit rather than by a man. As a result, Jesus did not inherit the fallen sinful nature of Adam, like every other human does. Jesus was completely without sin! He had God's Spirit *within* Him completely and perfectly, as had Adam and Eve before they sinned.

> *So it was, that while they [Mary and her betrothed, Joseph] were there [Bethlehem], the days were completed for her to be delivered [give birth]. And she brought*

forth her firstborn Son, and wrapped Him in swaddling [bands of] cloths, and laid Him in a manger [cattle-feeding trough], because there was no room for them in the inn.

—Luke 2:6-7

And an angel of the Lord appeared to some shepherds tending their sheep out in the fields (Luke 2:8-12). He said to them,

Do not be afraid, for behold, I bring you good tidings of great joy which will be to all people. For there is born to you this day in the city of David [Bethlehem] a Savior, who is Christ [Messiah] the Lord.

—Luke 2:10-11

God even brought wise men—magi, astronomers—from a faraway land to bring homage to the Child (Matthew 2:1-11). And just to ensure that His people, the Jews, got the message, both a woman and a man confirmed the identity of Jesus when He was dedicated to God by Joseph and Mary in the Jewish Temple (Luke 2:25-38).

Thus God miraculously fulfilled His prophecies of the coming Messiah in an astounding way!

WHO JESUS REALLY IS

I want to make sure that you understand who this tiny little Baby really is. He is not an angel. He is not just another prophet. He is not just a great teacher. He is not just a great martyr. He is not just another human being. He is God, the Creator, manifesting (expressing) Himself to the world as a real human.

In the beginning was [already existing] the Word [Jesus], and the Word was with God, and the Word was God. He was in the beginning with God. All things were made through Him, and without Him nothing was made that was made. In Him was life, and the life was the light of men... And the Word became flesh and dwelt among us, and we beheld His glory, the glory as of the only begotten of the Father, full of grace and truth.
—John 1:1–4, 14

And without controversy great is the mystery of godliness [God-likeness]: God was manifested [communicated, revealed, demonstrated] in the flesh...
—1 Timothy 3:16

Jesus, the Christ, the Messiah is:

- The Great Creator giving Himself to us as a created Human.
- The Almighty God giving Himself to us as a helpless newborn Baby.
- The Heavenly Father giving Himself to us as an earthly Son.
- The God-Who-Inhabits-Eternity confining Himself to the limits of time and space.
- The Sovereign Lord giving Himself to us as a lowly Servant.
- The Lord of Glory giving Himself to us as One with no reputation.
- The King of Heaven giving Himself to us as a lowly Carpenter.
- The Holy God giving Himself to us as the Man without sin.

Jesus is called the *"last Adam"* and the *"heavenly Man"* (1 Corinthians 15:45, 49). The first Adam, before his fall, was a man with God's Spirit living *within* him in fullness. Jesus, the second Adam, also was a man who had God's Spirit *within* him completely and perfectly, because Jesus was without sin. Even though He was tempted, Jesus did not fall!

Beloved, do not believe every spirit, but test the spirits, whether they are of God; because many false prophets have gone out into the world. By this you know the Spirit of God: Every spirit that confesses [proclaims] that Jesus Christ has come in the flesh is of God, and every spirit that does not *confess [proclaim] that Jesus Christ has come in the flesh is not of God.*
—1 John 4:1-3 (emphasis added)

Jesus was truly God, and truly human. He did not come to us as a superhuman. He came right down on our level and lived among us for thirty-three years! Jesus went through the whole gamut of human experience: confinement in a womb for nine months; the trauma of human birth; the helplessness of a newborn baby; the years of being a toddler, a young child, a teenager, a young man, a carpenter, and then a mature man—all *without sin*!

JESUS FORESHADOWS THE NEW COVENANT

But it was not enough for Jesus to come to earth to live a normal human life, even without sin. God sent Jesus as our example, to be sure, but also as a sacrifice for our sin.

We have seen that God sacrificed animals to make a covering for Adam and Eve's nakedness. Then we saw how God instituted animal sacrifices to cover the sins of His people. However, the sacrifices did not change the hearts of people. God established the Old Covenant with His people through animal sacrifices as an interim measure, a temporary, Band-Aid solution to the real problem.

God wanted to address the real problem, the heart issue—literally, the issue with our human hearts—so He established the New Covenant by sacrificing His own Son for our sins. Jesus came to live but also to die as the Sacrificial Lamb, in order to institute the New Covenant.

> *For He [God] made Him [Jesus] who knew no sin* to be *sin for us, that we might become the righteousness of God in Him.*
> —2 Corinthians 5:21 (emphasis added)

Many times during His life, Jesus Himself prophesied His sacrificial death. At His last meal, He specifically told His disciples that His death would establish the New Covenant promised by God. This occurred on the evening before His crucifixion, when Jesus ate the Passover meal with His twelve disciples (Matthew 26:20, 26-29; Mark 14:17, 22-25; Luke 22:14-20).

At that meal, Jesus took the unleavened bread, broke it, gave it to the disciples, and said, *"Take, eat; this is My body"* (Matthew 26:26; Mark 14:22) and *"This is My body which is given [broken] for you"* (Luke 22:19; see also 1 Corinthians 11:23-24). Then He took the cup of wine, gave thanks, and gave it to them, saying, *"Drink from it, all of you. For this is My blood [symbolically and prophetically] of the new covenant, which is shed for many for the remission [forgiveness] of sins"* (Matthew 26:27-28; also see Mark 14:24-25; Luke 22:20; 1 Corinthians 11:25).

THE MESSIAH WAS CRUCIFIED FOR ALL OUR SINS

Because of our sin, Jesus willingly went through the horrible experience of being betrayed, forsaken, shamed, mocked, ridiculed, whipped, and blasphemed. Because of our sin, He was nailed to a cross, and hung there for six long, torturous hours. There, God *"laid on Him the iniquity of us all"* (Isaiah 53:6).

> *[Jesus] made Himself of no reputation, taking the form of a bondservant, and coming in the likeness of men. And being found in appearance as a man, He humbled Himself and became obedient to the point of death, even the death of the cross. Therefore God also has highly exalted Him and given Him the name which is above every name...*
>
> —Philippians 2:7-9

While Jesus' pierced and battered body lay in that cold tomb, His sinless soul atoned (paid) for all our sin, suffering unimaginable horrors in the depths of hell (Ephesians 4:9; Matthew 12:40). But after three days, God raised Him from the dead, victorious and triumphant (Matthew 28:1-8; Luke 24:1-8). The full atonement (payment, penalty) for the sins of the *whole* human race—past, present, and future—had been completed. Jesus died for you and me and every human being!

For by one offering He [Jesus] has perfected forever
those who are being sanctified [purified].
　　　　—Hebrews 10:14 (see also verses 10-17)

The great purpose of, and main reason for, God becoming flesh and dwelling among us was for Him to die and atone for the sins of the whole human race. You will recall that this was foreshadowed in the Garden of Eden, when God sacrificed animals to cover Adam and Eve. Christ's sacrificial death on that cross, and the battle He won while in the tomb, pays for *all* our sins, and enables God the Father to fully and gladly forgive us, to cleanse us from *all* unrighteousness, and to breathe His Spirit into us.

But if we walk in the light as He is in the light, we have
fellowship with one another, and the blood of Jesus
Christ His Son cleanses us from all sin.
　　　　　　　　　　　　　　—1 John 1:7

And when God raised Jesus from the dead, it meant that the price had been fully paid, and that our redemption was totally complete.

But this Man, after He had offered one sacrifice for sins
forever, sat down at the right hand of God...
　　　　　　　　　　　　—Hebrews 10:12

The Old Covenant was finished, and the New Covenant was established.

JESUS' DEATH MAKES THE NEW COVENANT POSSIBLE

When we, in simple childlike faith, *receive* Jesus and the salvation He purchased for us on the cross, we are immediately totally forgiven, declared righteous, washed as white as snow, clothed with the perfect righteousness of Jesus Christ, and given the gift of eternal life.

I use the phrase "clothed with the perfect righteousness of Jesus Christ" because God used clothing as prophetic symbolism, when He took the skins of animals to clothe Adam and Eve after they sinned (Genesis 3:21). God used this same symbolism in the Parable of the Prodigal Son. The first thing the father did after he embraced his lost son was to clothe him with his best robe and put sandals on his feet (Luke 15:20–23). So, too, God covers us when we turn to Him for salvation. God imputes (credits or accounts) righteousness to those who believe in Jesus (Romans 4:6–8, 22–25). God also freely justifies (declares righteous) all those who receive Him by faith (Acts 13:38–39; Romans 3:22–26).

At the same moment that we receive God's covering of salvation through Christ, the Holy Spirit of Jesus Christ enters us and unites with our human spirit, and we are reborn spiritually, from above, by the Holy Spirit (John 3:3–8). This is the New Covenant that God prophesied through Jeremiah and Ezekiel:

I will put My law in their minds, and write it on their hearts.
—Jeremiah 31:33

I will give you a new heart and put a new spirit within you... I will put My Spirit within you...
—Ezekiel 36:26–27

This is the beginning of the restoration of what Adam and Eve lost when they sinned in the Garden of Eden. The moment they sinned, the Holy Spirit of God had to depart from their spirits, leaving their spirits empty, lonely, and dead. But now, through the crucifixion and resurrection of Jesus Christ, the Messiah, God will again breathe His Spirit into those who *receive* Jesus, and they will become new creations spiritually. This is what Jesus meant when He said we must be *"born again"* or *"born of the Spirit"* (John 3:3, 8).

> *Therefore, if anyone is in Christ, he is a new creation;*
> *old things have passed [and are passing] away; behold,*
> *all things have become [and are becoming] new.*
> —2 Corinthians 5:17

The Holy Spirit within Us Is Part of the New Covenant

Jesus also made the astounding promise that the Holy Spirit would live within us. Just before Jesus died, after He shared the Passover supper with His disciples, He said to them,

> *And I will pray the Father, and He will give you another*
> *Helper [Strength-giver], that He may abide with you for-*
> *ever—the Spirit of truth, whom the world cannot receive,*
> *because it neither sees Him nor knows Him; but you*
> *know Him, for He dwells* with *you and will be* in *you.*
> —John 14:16-17 (emphasis added)

Later, the first time Jesus met with His disciples after His crucifixion and resurrection, He did something to them that was very significant and that fulfilled His own prophesy. After greeting them and showing them His pierced hands and side, He *breathed* on them, saying, *"Receive the Holy Spirit"* (John 20:22; see also John 20:19–21).

"Receive" is written in an immediate verb tense, not a future tense. This means that it happened to them immediately; they entered into the New Covenant that God had prophesied! Jesus had paid for their sins, and they were born again, from above. *"And He opened their understanding, that they might comprehend the Scriptures"* (Luke 24:45) and thereby learn from God and have intimate, inner relationship with God by His Spirit within them.

This is exactly what God did to Adam when He created him out of the dust of the earth. God breathed His Spirit into Adam and he became a living spiritual being, able to intimately commune with God (Genesis 2:7).

Now, everyone who sincerely repents (turns back to God) and in childlike faith *receives* the crucified, resurrected, and ascended Jesus as their Savior and Lord, will be born again by the Holy Spirit. The Holy Spirit will then *enter into* them, and they will *enter into* the New Covenant. This is what happened to me when I received Jesus at the age of seven and His Spirit came into me: I was born of the Spirit and received God's forgiveness and eternal life.

You, too, can be in this wonderful relationship with God through Jesus. *Receive* Him as your Savior and Lord! Invite Jesus and His Spirit to come into your spirit and make you new.

CHAPTER FIVE

GOD ALSO PROMISES A GREAT OUTPOURING OF HIS HOLY SPIRIT

GOD CONFIRMS HIS WORD

One time, my wife was out of town for a few days and I didn't feel like cooking supper. So I decided to go to a nearby pizza parlor to eat. I had been there before and knew that the front part was a pizza parlor and the back part was a bar. When I arrived, I saw that they had renovated and made the whole place into a bar where you could still order pizza. I decided to stay, and chose a table in the back corner. While waiting for my pizza to come, I observed all that was going on. It happened to be St. Patrick's Day, so some of the patrons were really "whooping it up," as we say in Calgary. I saw some drug-dealing, some sexual activity developing, drunkenness, and the beginnings of a few fights.

I said to God, "I have sure brought You into a sinful place. It must really disturb You."

Immediately I heard in my spirit, "Oh, it's not the sin that bothers Me most." Right away, I thought to myself that this must be the voice of satan, because God is a holy God! But God said, "What grieves My heart very greatly is not their sin, but their lostness! If they come to Me, I will forgive all their sins, and change their lives. But if they do not come to Me, they are lost to Me, and I am lost to them—both now and forever."

Through this experience, God confirmed to me a message I had heard from Him while reading a prophecy in the book of Joel; God's main concern and burning passion is the salvation of our souls. Let's take a look at that prophecy.

GOD REVEALS HIS HEART FOR US

I have said that in the Garden of Eden, God gave Adam and Eve a full measure of His Spirit. God not only walked with them and communed with them; He lived *in* them and *filled* them. Recall that this is what was lost when Adam and Eve sinned, and what God promised to restore.

Christ's death and resurrection restored us to relationship with God. When Jesus breathed the Spirit *into* His disciples, they received the Holy Spirit and were born again. But as with Adam and Eve, God wanted them to have not just a little bit of His Spirit but instead to be *filled to overflowing* with His Spirit. Now He wants to be *in* all people and have all people experience *His fullness*, not just speak to us through certain people—His prophets—as He had done between the time of Adam and Christ.

So God gave another great prophecy concerning His Holy Spirit in the Old Testament Scriptures, this time through the prophet Joel. The fulfillment of Joel's prophecy played a key role in the New Testament and in the early church, and continues to be of great importance in the church today.

THE PROPHECY OF JOEL

This is what God prophesied through the prophet Joel:

*And it shall come to pass afterward that I will pour
out My Spirit on all flesh [peoples]; your sons and your
daughters shall prophesy, your old men shall dream
dreams, your young men shall see visions. And also on
My menservants and on My maidservants I will pour
out My Spirit in those days.*

*And I will show wonders in the heavens and in
the earth: blood and fire and pillars of smoke. The sun
shall be turned into darkness, and the moon into blood,
before the coming of the great and awesome day of the
Lord. And it shall come to pass that whoever calls on
the name of the Lord shall be saved. For in Mount Zion
and in Jerusalem there shall be deliverance [salvation],
as the Lord has said, among the remnant whom the
Lord calls.*

—Joel 2:28-32

Notice the difference between what God said about His
Holy Spirit through Jeremiah and Ezekiel, and what God said
about His Holy Spirit through Joel. Jeremiah and Ezekiel prophesied that God would place His Spirit *within* us; Joel prophesied
that God would *pour out* His Spirit *on* us. This is like the difference between drinking a glass of water and being immersed by
water in a shower or a river.

The Setting of Joel's Prophecy

At the time of Joel's prophecy, the land of Judah was in a great
drought and had experienced an invasion of consuming locusts.
There was no harvest, which caused a great famine. This catas-
trophe had occurred because God's people had turned away

from Him and ceased obeying His commandments. So God called for the priests to sound the trumpet and call the people to gather together, to fast, mourn, and turn back to Him with all their heart (Joel 1:1–2:11).

God promises that if they do this, He will do marvelous things and send a great rain—the *"former rain"* and the *"latter rain in the first month"* (Joel 2:23)—and a great harvest. He will restore what the locusts have eaten, and there will be great abundance (Joel 2:12–27).

A CLOSER LOOK AT JOEL'S PROPHECY

Now let's take a closer look at the prophecy God spoke through Joel. You will notice that there are three parts to Joel's prophecy. We will look at the first two parts together, then the third part.

Parts One and Two: Outpourings of the Spirit and Judgment

The first part of the prophecy (Joel 2:28–29) predicts the great and glorious outpouring of God's Spirit on all peoples.

- God said that a time would come when He would *pour out* His Spirit. The phrase "pour out" indicates that God was promising to give a great measure of His Spirit, not just a little sprinkle:

  ▷ upon all flesh: meaning all peoples, both Jews and Gentiles (non-Jews), worldwide;
  ▷ upon young and old, and sons and daughters: I believe this means that God has a special outpouring of the Spirit in mind for the young, since they are mentioned twice;

> ▷ upon male and female: God does not discriminate based on gender (Galatians 3:28);
> ▷ upon rich and poor: nor does God discriminate based on our socioeconomic status (Acts 10:34).

- Then God promises to give people prophecies, dreams, and visions, which are different ways in which God speaks to us by the Spirit (see Chapter Two and 1 Corinthians 12:1, 4-11).

Since the fulfillment of the first part of Joel's prophecy includes God's Spirit being outpoured on all people, this means Jesus' church will be cleansed, revived, and filled to overflowing with the light and glory of God.

The second part of Joel's prophecy (2:30–31) predicts the outpouring of awesome and fearful judgments on the earth in the form of wonders in the heavens and the earth: blood, fire, and pillars of smoke; the sun turned into darkness; and the moon turned into blood. These negative signs are in stark contrast to the positive signs in Joel 2:28–29.

Many New Testament scriptures also describe the awful things that will happen in the last days before Christ's return. According to these scriptures, these judgments will result in perilous times, causing men's hearts to fail them for fear (Luke 21:5-26). People will demonstrate *"a form of godliness"* but deny its power, and evil people will grow worse and worse (2 Timothy 3:1-13).

Part Three: A Great Harvest of Lost Souls Coming to Christ

One day as I was praying and meditating on this prophecy, I heard the Lord say in my spirit, "What is the end of this prophecy? How does it finish?" Since I couldn't remember, I got my Bible and looked it up. This is how this great prophecy ends:

> *And it shall come to pass that whoever calls on the name of the LORD shall be saved. For in Mount Zion and in Jerusalem there shall be deliverance [salvation]...*
> —Joel 2:32

(Mount Zion and Jerusalem are symbolic of the church.)

Then God said to me, "This is the main thing I am after: *the salvation of lost souls.* I want many people, worldwide, to turn to Me for the salvation of their souls, the forgiveness of their sins, and the gift of eternal life. This is the main reason I am going to pour out My Spirit on all peoples, and at the same time also pour out the wonders in heaven and earth: blood, fire, smoke, the sun darkened, and the moon turned red. There will be a great harvest of lost souls coming to Jesus for salvation and eternal life," which will complete His church, His glorious Bride!

So a great harvest of lost souls is God's *ultimate* purpose for the last great outpouring of His Spirit! Both the positive and negative signs are intended to work towards the same end goal.

Then the Lord showed me how this would happen, using the verses in Isaiah 60:1-3:

> *Arise, shine; for your light has come! And the glory of the LORD is risen upon you. For behold, the darkness shall cover the earth, and deep darkness the people; but the LORD will arise over you, and His glory will be seen upon you. The Gentiles [unbelievers] shall come to your light, and kings to the brightness of your rising.*

In this passage, God says that He will cause His light and glory to rise and to shine from His people, His church. Although darkness will cover the earth and deep darkness will cover the nations, His glory will be seen upon His people. As a result, the Gentiles (non-Jews, symbolic of non-believers) in deep spiritual darkness will see His glory, and come out of their fear and darkness to the brightness of God's shining.

I imagine that it will look something like this: people in deep spiritual darkness, with catastrophes happening all around them, will be afraid and not know what to do. They will see God's people at peace in the midst of the traumatic events, shining forth His glory. This will cause many to say, "I must get what they have," and then turn to God.

Joel's astounding prophecy of immense proportions and great significance began to be fulfilled in the New Testament many hundreds of years later. But before we get to that, we need a clear understanding of Who the Holy Spirit is.

Chapter Six

Who Is the Holy Spirit?

This is an immense and important question!

The Lord Is One

Moses told the Israelites, *"Hear, O Israel: The Lord our God, the Lord is one! You shall love the Lord your God with all your heart, with all your soul, and with all your strength"* (Deuteronomy 6:4–5). Jesus Himself quoted this scripture, emphasizing the highest two commandments given by God (Mark 12:29–30).

Jesus also said to the Samaritan woman at the well, *"God is Spirit, and those who worship Him must worship in spirit and truth"* (John 4:24). And God says in 2 Corinthians 3:17, *"Now the Lord is the Spirit; and where the Spirit of the Lord is, there is liberty."*

Through this, I believe God is saying, "The great, eternal Creator-God is the Holy Spirit. And the Holy Spirit is the great, eternal Creator-God. They are one and the same."

So the Scriptures are very clear that God is one.

These Three Are One

But the Scriptures also clearly refer to God the Father, God the Son, and God the Holy Spirit.

WHO IS THE HOLY SPIRIT?   53

For there are three that bear witness in heaven: the Father, the Word [Jesus the Son], and the Holy Spirit; and these three are one.

—1 John 5:7

For many centuries, theologians have tried to understand and explain this great spiritual mystery. They call it the doctrine of the Trinity. I prefer to use the term "Tri-unity." Whatever the term, how can we understand the concept? Let me share an illustration that may help.

One day, I was teaching an interdenominational Bible study. The question about the Trinity came up. Without me thinking about it, the following illustration came clearly to my mind. Since I had never heard it before, I believe it was God's voice.

Imagine a family dinner. I am there along with my father, my children, and my wife. Although I'm just one person, I have three totally different love relationships and responsibilities to these three. We are all simultaneously relating with each other, but in different ways. As a son to my father, I give honor, gratitude, and love. As a father to my children, I give loving care, protection, and provision. As a husband to my wife, I give a special loving care and provision that is far different than the other love relationships. I'm just the one person with the same love, nature, and character, but it is expressed in three different roles. I believe God is like that.

The Father is God. The Son is God. The Holy Spirit is God. And these three are *one*—always in total harmony and agreement.

Another example is yourself. God created you in His image, and each of us is a "tri-unity": body, soul, and spirit. You are one person, but you have three different aspects to you.

Any of these examples is imperfect, since we're not capable of fully understanding or explaining God. However, they can help us as we seek to see God, howsoever dimly (1 Corinthians 13:12).

SOME SYMBOLS OF THE HOLY SPIRIT

Scripture uses several symbols for the Holy Spirit—breath/wind, fire/flames, water/rain, and a dove—each of which describes a different aspect of the Holy Spirit.

Breath/Wind

When God created Adam, the word "breath" is used as a symbol of His Holy Spirit being breathed into Adam's spirit (Genesis 2:7). God spoke to His people through Ezekiel, promising to cause "breath"—His Spirit—to enter into their dryness and resurrect them to new life (Ezekiel 37:1-14). Jesus "breathed" on His disciples and said, *"Receive the Holy Spirit"* (John 20:22).

Jesus also uses the word "wind" as a symbol of the Holy Spirit giving spiritual birth, the beginning of spiritual life when He speaks to Nicodemus, a religious man who was seeking truth (John 3:1-8). On the day of Pentecost, when Jesus filled His disciples with the promised Holy Spirit, there was the sound of a rushing mighty wind (Acts 2:1-4).

Fire/Flames

The disciples also had individual flames, *"as of fire,"* which sat on each one of them at Pentecost (Acts 2:3-4). John the Baptist had prophesied that Jesus would baptize (immerse) us with the Holy Spirit and with fire (Matthew 3:11-12; Luke 3:16-17).

The scene described by John is a threshing floor where the wheat is trampled and pounded to free it from the chaff that surrounds it. Then, if a wind is blowing, the wheat and chaff are thrown into the air so that the chaff will be blown away from the wheat. If there is no wind, the harvesters would wave large fans to blow away the chaff. This is a symbolic picture of the Holy Spirit, as a wind, purifying our lives. John the Baptist prophesied that the Holy Spirit, as unquenchable fire, would then burn the chaff.

Water/Rain

As we have seen, God prophesied through Joel that He would pour out His Spirit as a great "rain" on all peoples (Joel 2:23-29). Jesus also used the symbol of "water" for the Holy Spirit when He shouted in the Temple, *"If anyone thirsts, let him come to Me and drink. He who believes in Me, as the Scripture has said, out of his heart [innermost being] will flow rivers of living water"* (John 7:37-38). John, the Gospel writer, states that Jesus was speaking of the Holy Spirit when He said this (John 7:39).

Dove

As Jesus came up out of the water after being baptized, the heavens opened, and the Holy Spirit descended in bodily form like a "dove" upon Him, and remained on Him (Matthew 3:16; Luke 3:22; John 1:32-34).

When I think of a dove, I think of a pure white bird, which is very gentle. However, as we will see, the Holy Spirit and His work in our lives is both gentle and strong.

But before we get there, let's take a closer look at the work of the Spirit at Jesus' baptism.

CHAPTER SEVEN

JESUS, HIMSELF, RECEIVES THE FULLNESS AND POWER OF GOD'S SPIRIT

Although God has promised a great outpouring of His Spirit, it isn't something we obtain without opening ourselves to receive God's Spirit. How does this occur? Let us look at the example given to us by Jesus Himself.

JESUS INSISTS ON BEING BAPTIZED

When Jesus was about thirty years old, before He began His public ministry, He went to John the Baptist to be baptized by him. John baptized people for repentance and forgiveness of sins, by immersing them in the Jordan River. Multitudes of people came to John to be baptized. Among them was Jesus.

John and Jesus were relatives; their mothers were related (Luke 1:36). So John must have known Jesus and was familiar with Jesus' righteous and holy life. John's mother and father both received a prophecy about John and Jesus (Luke 1:5-17, 41-45). John probably knew about these prophecies, too.

So when Jesus came to John to be baptized, John objected, saying, "I need to be baptized by You! Why are You coming to me?" But Jesus responded, "Allow this to occur, so that we will fulfill what God planned" (see Matthew 3:14-15). So John baptized Him.

Even though Jesus was conceived by the Holy Spirit, had the Holy Spirit within Him, and was totally sinless, He insisted on being baptized in water. Why? In order to be filled with and empowered by God's Holy Spirit. Being baptized in water is an act symbolizing death, burial, and resurrection. By being baptized (immersed) in water, Jesus was foreshadowing and embracing, ahead of time, His own death, burial, and resurrection, for our salvation. And He set this as an example for us to be baptized as well.

The Spirit of God Descends upon Jesus

Now, let's look at the result of Jesus' step of obedience. Whenever God does an audio/visual demonstration, it is very important!

When He had been baptized, Jesus came up immediately from the water; and behold, the heavens were opened to Him, and He saw the Spirit of God descending like a dove and alighting upon Him. And suddenly a voice came from heaven, saying, "This is My beloved Son, in whom I am well pleased."
—Matthew 3:16–17

And John bore witness, saying, "I saw the Spirit descending from heaven like a dove, and He remained upon Him. I did not know Him, but He who sent me to baptize with water said to me, 'Upon whom you see the Spirit descending, and remaining on Him, this is He who baptizes with the Holy Spirit.' And I have seen and testified that this is the Son of God."
—John 1:32–34 (emphasis added)

JESUS IS FILLED WITH THE POWER OF THE SPIRIT

After Jesus was baptized and filled with the Spirit, you might think God would release Him into ministry immediately. Instead, God led Him into the wilderness.

> *Then Jesus, being filled with the Holy Spirit, returned from the Jordan [River] and was led by the Spirit into the wilderness, [to be] tempted for forty days by the devil.*
> —Luke 4:1–2 (emphasis added)

Jesus had the Spirit (as promised by Jeremiah and Ezekiel), but God had more for Him (as promised by Joel). God knew what Jesus would face: rejection, betrayal, temptation, and ultimately crucifixion. So He knew Jesus would need a *full measure* of the Spirit: to be immersed in a baptism of the Spirit and not just drink of the Spirit. In the wilderness, as Jesus overcame each temptation of satan, He grew in the power of the Spirit. Only at that point did God know He was ready to begin His ministry.

> *Then Jesus returned [from the wilderness] in the* pow-*er of the Spirit to Galilee, and news of Him went out through all the surrounding region. And He taught in their synagogues, being glorified by all.*
> —Luke 4:14–15 (emphasis added)

Through Jesus' obedience in being baptized, following the Spirit's leading into the wilderness, and steadfastly resisting the temptation of satan, He set a powerful example for all of us. Like Jesus, we are to be baptized (immersed) both in water and in the Holy Spirit and His power.

GOD WANTS TO FILL US WITH HIS SPIRIT

It is important to understand that God earnestly desires to fill us with His Spirit. We need not beg for it. God delights to give us His Spirit. It is His *astounding promise!*

> *If you then, evil as you are, know how to give good gifts [gifts that are to advantage] to your children,* how much more *will your heavenly Father* give the Holy Spirit *to those who ask* and continue to *ask Him!*
> —Luke 11:13, AMP (emphasis added)

We need not earn it. In fact, we *cannot* earn it. Everything we have from God is due solely to His great, eternal grace. *"And what do you have that you did not receive [as a gift]?"* (1 Corinthians 4:7).

It took the Spirit of God to teach me that lesson.

GOD HAD TO CORRECT ME

One day, I was driving alone in my car and feeling a great need to seek God for a fresh infilling of the Spirit. I said to myself, "When I get home, I'm going to get into my bedroom alone and wrestle with God until He blesses me, like Jacob did."

Immediately I heard, "No, it was the angel who wrestled with Jacob."

I thought to myself that this was not from God, because I knew that story very well—or at least thought I knew it. It bothered me, so when I got home I looked up the story. There it said, *"a Man wrestled with him [Jacob]"* (Genesis 32:24). That Man was God!

This greatly changed my thinking. Previously, I had thought I must wrestle a blessing out of a rather reluctant God. But I had it exactly backwards. It is an eager God who wants to wrestle a blessing into a rather reluctant me! Like Jacob, God had to bring me to a place of brokenness and helplessness.

God loved that old deceiving Jacob so much that He came and wrestled with him until he was broken and helpless. And then God healed Jacob, blessed him, and changed him from being a Jacob (meaning "deceiver/manipulator") to being an Israel (meaning "prince who rules with God"). God transformed him into a prince who rules with God. What an astounding grace!

Chapter Eight

Jesus Promises Us the Fullness and Power of God's Spirit

"Ask and keep on asking"

Throughout His three and a half years of ministry, Jesus taught the people to ask God for the Holy Spirit, and to expect God to give His Spirit to them. An example of this is found in Luke 11:9-13:

> So I say to you, ask, and it will be given to you; seek, and you will find; knock, and it will be opened to you. For everyone who asks receives, and he who seeks finds, and to him who knocks it will be opened. If a son asks for bread from any father among you, will he give him a stone? Or if he asks for a fish, will he give him a serpent instead of a fish? Or if he asks for an egg, will he offer him a scorpion? If you then, being evil, know how to give good gifts to your children, how much more will your heavenly Father give the Holy Spirit to those who ask Him!
>
> —Luke 11:9-13 (emphasis added)

In the original Greek text, the verb tense for "ask," "seek," and "knock" is present/progressive. So in order to give you the full meaning, I'm going to quote this scripture from the Amplified Version of the Bible:

> *So I say to you, Ask and keep on asking and it shall be given you; seek and keep on seeking and you shall find; knock and keep on knocking and the door shall be opened to you. For everyone who asks and keeps on asking receives; and he who seeks and keeps on seeking finds; and to him who knocks and keeps on knocking, the door shall be opened.*
> —Luke 11:9-10, AMP

WHAT TO ASK FOR

Jesus gives us an illustration of a good father giving good gifts to his children when they ask. What would Jesus have in mind for us to ask of the Father? Material goods? Personal advancement? Jesus gave only one example:

> *If you then, evil as you are, know how to give good gifts [gifts that are to advantage] to your children,* how much more *will your heavenly Father* give the Holy Spirit *to those who ask* and continue to *ask Him!*
> —Luke 11:13, AMP (emphasis added)

Jesus has encouraged us; let us ask for the Holy Spirit, knowing that God will answer our prayer.

KEEP ON DRINKING

Jesus reiterated this encouragement to us at another time in His ministry. This time, Jesus stood in the midst of God's Temple in Jerusalem and shouted, *"If anyone thirsts, let him come to Me and drink [and keep drinking]. He who believes in Me, as the Scripture has said, out of his heart will flow rivers of living water"* (John 7:37-38). The Gospel writer John tells us that Jesus said this concerning the Spirit, whom believers in Christ would receive, and that the Holy Spirit had not yet been given, since Jesus had not yet been glorified (not yet ascended) (John 7:39).

Every time I think of this verse, and come to Jesus to drink of His Spirit, the picture comes to my mind of God leading Israel out of slavery in Egypt and into the Sinai wilderness, which was very dry and barren. God provided manna—heavenly bread— every morning. He also provided a rock out of which flowed water for the whole multitude of His people. Every time Israel journeyed to a new camp, the rock was there, providing water. 1 Corinthians 10:4 says that Israel *"all drank the same spiritual drink. For they drank of that spiritual Rock that followed them, and that Rock was Christ."*

God still pours His Spirit out for us today, wherever we are! Even if you find yourself in a spiritual wilderness, a dry and barren land, God's Spirit, through Jesus, will flow out to you to refresh you and satisfy your spiritual thirst.

WHY THE GIFT OF THE HOLY SPIRIT IS SO IMPORTANT

Just before Jesus was about to be betrayed and crucified, He ate the last supper with His disciples. At that Passover meal, He told them that He was going back to the Father, and He promised to send them the Holy Spirit, the Helper, the Comforter (Strength-giver).

> *And I will pray the Father, and He will give you an-other Helper [Strength-giver], that He may abide with you forever... It is to your advantage that I go away; for if I do not go away, the Helper [Strength-giver] will not come to you; but if I depart, I will send Him to you.*
> —John 14:16; 16:7

Notice that Jesus told His disciples that it was to their advantage that He would leave them. This must have been very surprising to them. How could this have been an advantage?

Well, if Jesus had stayed on the earth physically, there would be only a limited number of people who could see Him, hear Him, touch Him, or be healed by Him on any given day. By going away, He sends His Spirit into *everyone* who receives Him, and fills them with His nature, His presence, and His power. So now, millions of people around the world every day can simul-taneously, personally hear Him, speak with Him, commune in-timately and lovingly with Him, grow in their relationship with Him, and be powerfully used by Him. What a wonderful and astounding advantage that is for every one of us!

WHAT DOES THE GIFT OF THE HOLY SPIRIT MEAN?

Jesus not only promised the Holy Spirit would come to us; He also described to us what that would mean. At the Passover supper, Jesus spoke of seven main things the Holy Spirit would do when Jesus sent Him to us in His fullness and power (John 14:25-16:15):

- He will help and comfort (strengthen) you, and abide with you.
- He will teach you all things.
- He will testify of Jesus.
- He will convict the world of sin, righteousness, and judgment.
- He will guide you into all truth, because He will speak whatever He hears from the Father.
- He will tell you things to come.
- He will glorify Jesus.

Later on, after Jesus' crucifixion and resurrection, and just before He ascended into heaven, He repeated the promise He had made to His disciples, and described how the Spirit would give us power, especially the power to witness to unsaved people (Acts 1:1-9).

Notice that Jesus used several different terms to describe the fullness and power of the Holy Spirit. He spoke of the Helper, the Comforter or Strength-giver, the Spirit of Truth, the Promise of the Father, the baptism with the Holy Spirit, and the outpouring of the Holy Spirit. Each term expresses a different aspect of the work of the Spirit in our lives. Here are a few examples to illustrate the impact and influence the Holy Spirit can have on us.

The Holy Spirit as Helper

Most assuredly, I say to you, he who believes in Me, the works that I do he will do also; and greater works than

these he will do, because I go to My Father... And I will pray the Father, and He will give you another Helper [Strength-giver], that He may abide with you forever.
—John 14:12, 16

At the creation of the world, God said that it was not good for Adam to be alone, so God created Eve as a companion for him. Thus, Adam and Eve were to support and encourage each other physically and emotionally.

Spiritually, Adam and Eve were supported and encouraged by God Himself. So, too, we are to be supported and encouraged by the Holy Spirit as a Helper or Strength-giver. Paul prayed that we would be strengthened through the Spirit in our inner beings (Ephesians 3:16). And we are also to be a supporter and encourager to each other in the body of Christ.

The Holy Spirit as Teacher

[T]he Holy Spirit, whom the Father will send in My name, He will teach you all things, and bring to your remembrance all things that I said to you.
—John 14:26

The Holy Spirit will open our understanding to enable us to comprehend the Scriptures (Luke 24:45; 1 Corinthians 2:9-14; 1 John 2:27). He will also speak directly and personally to our spirits and minds, teaching us, guiding us, and training us.

The Holy Spirit helped the early disciples to remember the things Jesus had said and done. This enabled the writers of the four Gospels—Matthew, Mark, Luke, and John—to be inspired by the Holy Spirit to accurately write these four Gospels as divine Scripture, the beginning of the New Testament Scriptures we have today.

The Holy Spirit Will Testify of Jesus

But when the Helper [Strength-giver] comes, whom I shall send to you from the Father, the Spirit of truth who proceeds from the Father, He will testify of Me.
—John 15:26

The Holy Spirit will progressively reveal to us the truth about Jesus, the Messiah: who He really is; what His life on earth was really like; what He accomplished by His crucifixion, burial, resurrection, and glorious ascension to the highest throne in heaven; and His return for us, His church. Through the Spirit, God reveals to us the things God has prepared for those who love Him (1 Corinthians 2:9-10).

The Holy Spirit Will Convict the World

And when He [the Holy Spirit] has come, He will convict the world of sin, and of righteousness, and of judgment.
—John 16:8

Through the apostle Paul, God has revealed that the god-of-this-age (satan) has blinded the minds of those who do not believe, so that they do not comprehend the gospel. But God will command the light of the knowledge and glory of God to shine into their minds and hearts, and dispel their blindness (2 Corinthians 4:3-6).

The Holy Spirit will not convict of sin, righteousness, and judgment just to make people feel miserable. He does this to lead them to repentance and salvation. This is God's heart for them.

This great conviction leading to great repentance must first begin at the household of God, us Christians (1 Peter 4:17). And oh, how we need it!

The Holy Spirit Will Guide Us into Truth

However, when He, the Spirit of truth, has come, He will guide you into all truth; for He will not speak on His own authority, but whatever He hears [from the Father] He will speak.

—John 16:13

The Holy Spirit is the Spirit of Truth. As such, the Holy Spirit is able to guide us into all truth. Jesus said that all the Father has is His, and promised to declare all of that to us through His Spirit (John 16:15). All the riches of God in Christ Jesus are beyond human comprehension (Ephesians 3:20). But the Holy Spirit will reveal more and more of this to us as we mature.

The Spirit will speak to us personally in our hearts. We must expect this and seek to recognize His voice more and more. How will this occur? He will speak to us through the written Word of God. He also will speak to us through pastors, teachers, and other fellow Christians (Ephesians 4:11-12; Ephesians 5:18-19; Colossians 3:16). Let's learn to listen—and listen, to learn.

The Holy Spirit Will Tell Us Things to Come

He [the Holy Spirit] will tell you things to come.

—John 16:13

God spoke through the many prophets in the Old Testament. These prophets spoke not only to their present conditions, but they also foretold future events, including the coming of Jesus, the Messiah. Jesus, while He was still on earth, also foretold many things that would happen in the future, such as the destruction of the Temple in Jerusalem (Matthew 24:1-2).

Jesus also gave to His New Testament church the gift of prophecy, which is one of the many gifts of the Holy Spirit (1 Corinthians 12:1, 4-11). In this way, the Spirit sometimes tells us things to come.

The Holy Spirit Will Glorify Jesus

[The Holy Spirit] will glorify Me [Jesus], for He will take of what is Mine and declare it to you. All things that the Father has are Mine. Therefore I said that He will take of Mine and declare it to you.

—John 16:14-15

The Holy Spirit will give to Jesus all glory, honor, praise, and exaltation. Jesus is the Head of His body, the church, and He must be first in every way, in all things (Colossians 1:18-19).

No matter how greatly God may bless us and use us, we must never glorify and exalt ourselves! We must give to Jesus all the credit, praise, honor, and glory. Otherwise it will be selfish pride and idolatry!

The Holy Spirit Will Empower Us

Behold, I send the Promise of My Father upon you; but tarry [wait] in the city of Jerusalem until you are endued [invested] with power from on high.

—Luke 24:49 (emphasis added)

But you shall receive power *when the Holy Spirit has come upon you; and you shall* be witnesses *to Me in Jerusalem, and in all Judea and Samaria, and to the end of the earth.*

—Acts 1:8 (emphasis added)

Jesus, through the baptism of the Holy Spirit, will give us His supernatural (beyond human) power from heaven. The Holy Spirit will give us the power to be effective witnesses, in life and in word, to the unsaved people around us, of Jesus' wonderful love and salvation. He will give us the loving, humble boldness to lead people to receive Christ—and then to disciple them.

THE HOLY SPIRIT SEALS THE PRESENCE AND PROMISES OF GOD

As we have seen, God promises to give us the Holy Spirit to dwell in us. And the presence of the Holy Spirit within us confirms our son/daughter relationship with God.

The Spirit Himself bears witness with our spirit that we are children of God, and if children, then heirs—heirs of God and joint heirs with Christ...

—Romans 8:16-17

The Lord Jesus seals us with His stamp of genuine ownership, and gives us the Spirit in our hearts as a deposit—a down-payment or guarantee—of much more to come: the inheritance we have in God (2 Corinthians 1:21-22; 2 Corinthians 5:5; Ephesians 1:13-14). The Holy Spirit also seals us for the day of redemption, when we will go to be with the Lord (Ephesians 4:30).

EXAMPLES OF THE HOLY SPIRIT WORKING IN ME

I can personally testify that right after I received the baptism of the Holy Spirit, these things Jesus promised the Holy Spirit would do really did begin to happen more and more. His astounding promises are true! Here are two examples of how the Holy Spirit taught me, convicted me, and guided me into truth.

God Teaches and Guides Us in the Details of Daily Life

One time I heard a couple of Spirit-filled preachers teach on godly marriage. They taught that a husband should love his wife *"just as Christ also loved the church and gave Himself"* for it by laying down His life (Ephesians 5:25). They also taught that husbands should *"love their own wives as [they love] their own bodies"* (Ephesians 5:28); and care for her, cherish her, and honor her, *"just as the Lord [Christ] does the church"* (Ephesians 5:29; see also Colossians 3:19; 1 Peter 3:7).

This was quite new to me, and it sounded very spiritual. Up to that time, the only teaching I had heard was, "Wives submit, wives submit," which is only one side of the coin. I wrestled with this teaching for a bit, and then said to the Lord, "Yes, I will love my wife, Reta, and lay down my life for her." I felt that I was doing a noble and very spiritual thing.

Then I heard the Lord say to me very clearly, "Humph! You won't even lay down your newspaper for her." Right away, I knew what He meant.

Many times, when I would read the newspaper, Reta would think of something to say to me. I would keep my head buried in the newspaper until she finally got my attention. Then, when she was finished speaking, I would wait for a few moments to make sure she was finished. Then I would pick up the newspaper again. However, many times something else would come to her mind, which she wanted to tell me. And I would try to keep my head buried in the newspaper until, a bit disgruntled, I reluctantly put down the newspaper and listened to her. Sometimes this scenario was repeated several times in a row. I don't think Reta was doing this on purpose.

This may seem a bit humorous and trivial, but God was emphasizing to me that our submission and obedience to Him must reach into the small details of our daily lives. He was also dealing with my spiritual pride and selfishness. What a wonderful God we have!

God Said, "Ask the Judge to forgive them"

This happened to me when I was on a walk alone. I had been very active in the charismatic movement. A few of the people to whom I had ministered, and in whom I had trusted, had turned against me. This hurt me deeply. However, I knew that one of Jesus' main commandments was to forgive those who have sinned against you (Matthew 6:14-15; Matthew 18:21-35). So I said to the Lord, "I forgive them, Lord." I thought I was doing something quite spiritual.

But in the back of my mind, I also had this thought: "We are all going to stand before the judgment seat of Christ and give account for what we have done and said. They will get it then."

Then I heard God say, "Ask the Judge to forgive them, just like Jesus did."

Immediately I remembered what Jesus had said while nailed on that cross, in great pain, after being horribly rejected, whipped, and blasphemed; Jesus said, *"Father, forgive them, for they do not know what they do"* (Luke 23:34). He asked the Father, who is the supreme Judge of heaven and earth, to forgive those who had rejected and crucified Him, of the horrible thing they were doing to Him.

I also remembered what Stephen said, as he was being stoned to death. He cried out with a loud voice, *"Lord, do not charge them with this sin"* (Acts 7:60).

This is like saying to a judge here on earth, "I withdraw the charges. Cancel the court case." All this was a great revelation to me. I knew that I had to wholeheartedly forgive those who had turned against me. And I did.

A few days after this, a young woman was brought to me for counseling. She was having a deep struggle and getting nowhere. As a young girl, two of her uncles had sexually abused her. After she had accepted Christ, she confided this to her counselors and pronounced that she forgave her uncles. But she did not get any release, or freedom, or peace. With the revelation God had just given to me, I encouraged her to ask God, the Judge, to forgive both her uncles and withdraw all charges against them. As soon as she did this, she was freed from all the guilt, shame, and depression she had been experiencing. From that time onwards, she became a shining, effective witness for

Jesus Christ.

Since then, I have seen the same results many times when people applied this principle of asking God, the Judge, to forgive those who have sinned against them.

CHAPTER NINE

GOD BEGINS TO FULFILL HIS ASTOUNDING PROMISE

THE FIRST GREAT OUTPOURING OF HIS ASTOUNDING PROMISE

The Context

Before Jesus' ascension into heaven,

> *He commanded them [His apostles] not to depart from Jerusalem, but to wait for the Promise of the Father, "which," He said, "you have heard from Me; for John truly baptized with water, but you shall be* baptized with the Holy Spirit *not many days from now... But you shall receive* power *when the Holy Spirit has come upon you; and you shall* be witnesses *to Me in Jerusalem, and in all Judea and Samaria, and to the end of the earth."*
>
> —Acts 1:4–5, 8 (emphasis added)

After Jesus' ascension into heaven, the disciples returned to Jerusalem with great joy, and were frequently in the Temple, praising God (Luke 24:51-53). They stayed together in an upper room with Mary the mother of Jesus, His brothers, and others; about 120 in total (Acts 1:13-15). They must have been joyfully expecting, asking for, and waiting for the astounding promise of the fullness and power of the Holy Spirit that Jesus had promised.

The Outpouring

Ten days after Jesus ascended into heaven was the Jewish Feast of Pentecost, which is also called the Feast of Harvest. "Pentecost" means fifty days, and this feast occurred fifty days after Christ's resurrection. On this feast day, God's promise of the Holy Spirit's fullness and power was fulfilled in an astounding way:

> When the Day of Pentecost had fully come, they were all with one accord in one place. And suddenly there came a sound from heaven, as of a rushing mighty wind, and it filled the whole house where they were sitting. Then there appeared to them divided tongues, as of fire [like individual flames], and one [flame] sat [rested] upon each of them. And they were all filled with the Holy Spirit and began to speak with other tongues [languages], as the Spirit gave them utterance.
>
> —Acts 2:1–4

The sound of this rushing mighty wind drew a great crowd from the city of Jerusalem. In this crowd were people from many different nations. They heard these Jewish believers speaking in their various native languages about the wonderful works of God. Some were amazed and perplexed, but others thought the disciples were drunk (Acts 2:5–13).

In response, Peter told them the disciples were not drunk. After all, it was only 9:00 in the morning! Instead, they were witnessing

what was spoken by the prophet Joel: "And it shall come to pass in the last days, *says God, that I will pour out of My Spirit on all flesh [peoples]; your sons and your daughters shall prophesy, your young men shall see visions, your old men shall dream dreams. And on My menservants and on My maidservants I will pour out My Spirit in those days; and they shall prophesy."*
> —Acts 2:16–18 (emphasis added)

On All Peoples

This outpouring of God's Holy Spirit was one of God's greatest audio/visual demonstrations! Notice that God's promise of the Holy Spirit through Joel was to all peoples:

- Every person—men and women
- Every age—young and old
- Every class—menservants and maidservants

Notice, too, that what Joel prophesied is exactly what happened to the disciples: they *all* were filled with the Holy Spirit—not just the apostles, but *all*, both men and women. God's astounding promise of the fullness and power of the Holy Spirit is available to all believers in Jesus Christ, male and female, young and old, in every ethnic group, all over the world!

An Object Lesson on "All Peoples"

So that the disciples would understand what He meant by "all peoples," God demonstrated the message by giving them an object lesson through a Roman soldier.

A Roman citizen named Cornelius lived in the city of Caesarea. He was a Centurion (an officer in charge of a hundred soldiers). He was a devout man and prayed to God always, although he was not a Jew. Both he and his family feared (reverenced) God.

God gave Cornelius a vision of an angel. The angel commanded Cornelius to send for the apostle Peter, who was staying in a nearby town.

The next day, God gave the apostle Peter a vision which was repeated three times, in which God said to Peter each time, *"What God has cleansed [made clean] you must not call common [unclean]"* (Acts 10:15). While Peter was wondering what this meant, the men from Cornelius arrived and asked Peter to come with them. The Holy Spirit said to Peter, "Go with them, and don't wonder about it, for I have sent them" (see Acts 10:1-20).

Notice that God had to give Cornelius a vision of an angel in order for him to call for Peter. God also had to give Peter a *triple* vision to get him to come into a Gentile's home. Why? Because the Jews had developed their own strict custom never to stay in a Gentile's house or eat with a Gentile.

Peter went with the men and found Cornelius waiting. Despite the Jewish custom, Cornelius had faith that Peter would come, and had called together his relatives and close friends as well. So when Peter went in, he found many who had come together. Then he said to them, "You know that it's against Jewish law for me to be with someone who is not a Jew. But God showed me that I should not consider anyone to be beyond God's love. So I came without protest as soon as I was sent for. But why did you send for me?" (see Acts 10:21-29)

Cornelius explained to Peter about the vision he had received from God. Peter must have been astounded to hear what he had to say, since it lined up perfectly with the visions God had given Peter. God was teaching Peter a lesson. And Peter learned quickly, for he then said, "Now I understand that God shows no favorites, but everyone who loves and follows Him is accepted by Him" (see Acts 10:30-35).

Then Peter preached to them:

- peace with God through Jesus Christ;
- that Jesus is Lord of all;
- that God anointed Jesus with the Holy Spirit and power;
- that God was with Jesus, doing good, healing, and setting people free from satan's power;
- that Jesus was crucified for all our sins;
- that God raised Jesus from the dead;
- that Jesus was ordained by God to be the Judge of the living and the dead; and
- that whoever believes in Jesus will receive forgiveness of sins (see Acts 10:36-43).

While Peter was still preaching, the Holy Spirit fell upon everyone who heard him. The Jews who had come with Peter were astounded, for they heard these Gentiles praise God and speak with different languages, just as the Jewish believers had done on the day of Pentecost. Then they knew that the gift of the Holy Spirit had been poured out on the Gentiles also.

Peter asked how anyone could argue against these people being baptized, since they had received the Holy Spirit, just as the Jews had received the Holy Spirit and been baptized. So he commanded them to be baptized in the name of the Lord Jesus (Acts 10:44-48).

Now when the apostles and believers back in Judea heard

that Gentiles had been converted and received the Holy Spirit, they couldn't believe it. When Peter returned, they even argued with Peter about it. Peter told them everything that had happened and finished by saying, "If God gave them the same gift as He gave us when we believed on the Lord Jesus Christ, who was I to argue with God?" When they heard that, they had nothing to say. Instead they praised God, saying, "Then God has *also* given the Gentiles the gift of repentance to eternal life" (see Acts 11:1-18).

This was a significant turning point for the church, since to that point only Jews had come to faith in Christ. It helped the believers in the early church to realize that God's astounding love, the astounding sacrifice of His beloved Son on the cross, and the astounding promise of the fullness and the power of His Holy Spirit, is

for every man and woman,
for every boy and girl,
of every nation, tribe, and tongue,
on all this planet earth.

THE POWER OF THE HOLY SPIRIT

We have seen that the astounding promise of God's Spirit is for all. But what is the result when people are filled with the Holy Spirit? Let's look at some examples from the New Testament.

Boldness

When Peter was filled with the Holy Spirit on the day of Pentecost, he was filled with great, loving boldness. It was apparent that many of the people in the crowd had demanded the crucifixion of Jesus. Even though they could have demanded that Peter also be crucified, Peter confronted the crowd and challenged them, saying,

Jesus of Nazareth, a Man attested [proved] by God to you by miracles, wonders, and signs which God did through Him in your midst, as you yourselves also know—Him, being delivered by the determined purpose and foreknowledge of God, you have taken by lawless hands, have crucified, and put to death; whom God raised up, having loosed [destroyed] the pains of death, because it was not possible that He should be held by it.

—Acts 2:22-24

Then Peter quoted the prophet David

concerning the resurrection of the Christ [Messiah], that His soul was not left in Hades, nor did His flesh see corruption. This Jesus God has raised up, of which we are all witnesses. Therefore being exalted to the right hand of God, and having received from the Father the promise of the Holy Spirit, He poured out this which you now see and hear. For David did not ascend into the heavens, but he says himself: "The LORD said to my Lord, 'Sit at My right hand, till I make Your enemies Your footstool.'" Therefore let all the house of Israel know assuredly that God has made this Jesus, whom you crucified, both Lord and Christ [Messiah].

—Acts 2:31-36

Conviction of Sin and Repentance

Now when the crowd heard this, they were deeply convicted and asked Peter and the other apostles what they should do. Peter responded,

> Repent, and let every one of you be baptized in the name of Jesus Christ for the remission [forgiveness] of sins; and you shall receive the gift of the Holy Spirit. For the promise is to you and to your children, and to all who are afar off, as many as the Lord our God will call.
>
> —Acts 2:38-39

Conversions

Everyone who received Peter's message was baptized. As a result, the number of believers grew by about three thousand that day (Acts 2:41). On another occasion, after God performed some miracles, the number of believers increased to about five thousand men (Acts 4:4), which may not have included women and children.

> And the Lord added to the church daily those who were being saved.
>
> —Acts 2:47 (emphasis added)

> And believers were increasingly added to the Lord, multitudes of both men and women...
>
> —Acts 5:14

Love and Unity Among the Believers

Perhaps the greatest sign of the work of the Holy Spirit in the early church was the love and unity among the believers. All of the believers lived in close relationship with one another, continuing in prayer under the teaching of the apostles (Acts 2:42–47).

> *Now all who believed were together, and had all things in common, and sold their possessions and goods, and divided them among all, as anyone had need. So continuing daily with one accord in the temple, and breaking bread from house to house, they ate their food with gladness and simplicity [sincerity] of heart, praising God and having favor with all the people.*
> —Acts 2:44–47

Miracles

Some days later, when Peter and John were entering the Temple, God used them to heal a man who had been lame since birth.

> *…and many wonders and signs were done through the apostles.*
> —Acts 2:43

> *And believers were increasingly added to the Lord, multitudes of both men and women, so that they brought the sick out into the streets and laid them on beds and couches, that at least the shadow of Peter passing by might fall on some of them. Also a multitude gathered*

*from the surrounding cities to Jerusalem, bringing sick
people and those who were tormented by unclean spirits, and they were all healed.*

—Acts 5:14-16

Continued Witness under Threats

Although the believers won favor with the people generally,
some religious leaders were threatened by what was occurring.
They arrested the disciples, telling them to stop preaching Jesus
(Acts 4:1-21). However, instead of giving in, the believers remained steadfast in their witness of Christ, praying,

*Now, Lord, look on their threats, and grant to Your ser-
vants that with all boldness they may speak Your word,
by stretching out Your hand to heal, and that signs and
wonders may be done through the name of Your holy
Servant Jesus.*

—Acts 4:29-30

After they prayed, the place where they were gathered to-
gether was shaken and they were all filled with the Holy Spirit.
As a result, they spoke the Word of God boldly and with great
power preached the resurrection of the Lord Jesus (Acts 5:31).
"And great grace was upon them all" (Acts 4:33). God confirmed
His presence with them!

THE ASTOUNDING PROMISE IS A GIFT

I must emphasize something that is very important. The Holy
Spirit said through Peter, on the day of Pentecost, that the *gift*

of the fullness and power of the Holy Spirit would be given to all who repented, received Jesus Christ as Savior and Lord, and were baptized (Acts 2:38–39). God called His astounding promise a *gift*. It cannot be earned, worked for, or deserved. Even some of the murderers of Jesus received this from God as a free gift! It is by God's free grace, and grace means it is a free gift.

God taught me this in a very clear way. I was once in a church and we were singing a hymn that went like this: "Oh, to grace, how great a debtor, daily I'm constrained to be." Instantly I heard God say, "No, My grace is not a debt. It is a totally *free* gift. It is not a loan, nor a mortgage. It cannot be deserved or earned. It cannot be paid back. It must be received by faith as a totally free gift—with eternal gratitude."

I was shocked. I thought to myself that this must not be the Lord. When I got home, I looked up the words "debt" and "debtor" in a Bible concordance, and found that the words I had heard had really come from the Lord. The Scriptures mention us being debtors only to the unsaved people around us, to tell them the gospel of Jesus Christ (Romans 1:14). This revelation deepened my love for, my worship of, and my gratitude to my Lord.

Every person on earth can now freely receive, from God, by His great grace, what Adam and Eve lost when they sinned! How utterly and gloriously astounding this is for God's whole dark, sinful, lost world!

CHAPTER TEN

GOD'S ASTOUNDING PROMISE
IS FOR US—NOW

God's astounding promise of the Holy Spirit did not end at the last chapter of the book of Acts. Nor did it end at the close of the first century. It was never rescinded! As we have seen, it was, and is, an integral part of the New Covenant given to us in Jesus Christ. A covenant is much more binding than a promise, and God *never* breaks His promises or His covenants.

SATAN ATTACKS, BUT GOD REVIVES

The early church—the body of believers after Jesus' resurrection and ascension—were beautifully loving, united, powerful, and fruitful. They were not perfect or sinless, but the salvation of Christ's death and resurrection, along with the fullness and power of the baptism of the Holy Spirit, had greatly and beautifully transformed them for God's glory. This was the glorious beginning of the fulfillment of God's astounding promise through the prophet Joel (Joel 2:28-32).

But satan began to attack the church in many vicious and subtle ways. Many in the church—both leaders and members—eventually turned away from God. It takes only a quick look through church history to see how greatly our enemy has changed and twisted God's precious church, His family, the body of Christ which is His bride, and how often His church has fallen short of Jesus' teachings.

But no matter what our enemy has done to Christ's church throughout the centuries, and no matter how far the church has fallen from God's ways, God has continued to speak to His people to draw them to Himself, just as He did from the time of Adam until Christ. Throughout church history, there have been revivals, outpourings of the Holy Spirit, large and small, from time to time, in various places and in various ways, as people responded to God's Spirit. I think this is what God meant when He said that times of refreshing and the times of restoration would come from the presence of the Lord (Acts 3:19-21).

Some of the more well-known revivals were led by Martin Luther, John Calvin, and John Wesley, which greatly reformed and transformed the church. There were the first and second awakenings in the United States. In the early nineteenth century, there were the Welsh revival and the Azusa Street revival in Los Angeles, which started the present-day Pentecostal movement.

These are but a few of many outpourings of the Holy Spirit throughout church history. Some of these affected whole nations, and others just a region, town, or congregation. Many times throughout church history, God has filled individuals with His Holy Spirit. So from the day of Pentecost until this present day, God has made His astounding promise available for everyone who has personally received the crucified, resurrected, ascended Christ as their Savior and Lord.

THE CHARISMATIC MOVEMENT

In the latter part of the 1950s, God began to pour out the fullness of His Spirit upon many people and churches of a wide variety of denominations, in great numbers, and in many places around the world. This was not organized by any person, organization, or denomination. I have never heard of anything like it in all of church history. Hundreds of thousands of people around the world were born again and baptized to overflowing with the Holy Spirit.

People eventually called it the "charismatic movement," because of the many gifts of the Spirit and miraculous signs that accompanied it. *Charisma* is the Greek word for "gift." This word is used in 1 Corinthians 12:4-11 and Romans 12:4-8 to refer to the gifts of the Holy Spirit. So the movement was named after the gifts being given by God to many of the people involved.

But this movement of the Holy Spirit was about much more than the gifts of the Spirit. It was also about nominal Christians being born again and baptized in the Holy Spirit. Lukewarm Christians were filled with love, joy, unity, and a passion and power to witness to people and lead them to receive Christ. All this happened in small home groups, Bible studies, churches big and small, conferences, and even large sports stadiums.

I can't help but believe, and eagerly hope, that this movement of the Holy Spirit was simply the foretaste of, and preparation for, a much greater, purer, fuller, and final great outpouring of God's Spirit before Jesus returns for His church, His precious bride. Jesus has promised to come for a glorious bride, holy and without fault in the eyes of God (Ephesians 5:25-27).

MY OWN PERSONAL EXPERIENCE

I have shared how God brought me down from my self-confidence, self-effort, and human-striving, when I was serving Him with *my* power but, unwittingly, without *His* great power. I also had a pride and striving for success, which I was not aware of at the time.

It was in my second five-year term in India. I was the director of Bombay Youth for Christ, and also the interim pastor of the Bombay Baptist Church. But God, in His great love and mercy, whittled me down to where I was spiritually very dry, empty, powerless, hungry, and thirsty. I couldn't get much from reading my Bible, I could hardly pray, and I was having great difficulty thinking of sermons to preach. This happened in the early 1960s.

A Ray of Hope in the Darkness

About that time, I came across quite a few articles in Christian magazines and periodicals about how the Holy Spirit had come to churches of various denominations and in many places. I read how God had made such great and beautiful transformations in so many individuals and congregations. The accounts made my heart burn within me and gave me some hope for my personal relationship with God.

Also about that time, I came across a few missionaries who were from different countries and denominations, and who were beautifully and genuinely filled with the Holy Spirit. My wife and I became friends with some of them, and could see in their lives and ministries something we did not have.

I Became Convinced

I had to struggle with some of my theological positions and denominational prejudices about all this.[1] So I looked into the

---

1 Not all Christian denominations believe that the Holy Spirit is actively at work in this way today.

Word of God and found that what these Christians had experienced, and were experiencing, was truly scriptural.

I began to hunger and thirst, to yearn and burn in my heart, for the baptism and fullness of the Holy Spirit. At first I prayed for God to fill me, but not with tongues. The Lord reproved me for dictating terms to Him. I said reluctantly, "Okay Lord, with tongues if You insist." Then the Lord reproved me for my reluctance. He finally brought me to the place where I was completely willing and eager for all that He had for me.

I became so convinced that I began to preach this in the church, explaining to the people that I hadn't yet had this experience, but it was in the Scriptures and we needed it. I also started a weekly home prayer meeting at which we prayed for God to give His astounding promise to us and to our church. A few of the church people began to attend, and we prayed week after week, asking, and continuing to ask, for God to pour out His Spirit as He had promised in His Word.

The Lord Sent Us a Spirit-Filled Man of God

I began to hear of David McKee, an Irish Presbyterian missionary who lived in the state next to Bombay. David was a Christ-centered, Spirit-filled, godly man with a fruitful and powerful ministry that included some of the manifestations of the Holy Spirit I had read about. Eventually, I had the opportunity to meet him. I told him about Bombay Baptist Church and how some of us were praying for God to come and fill us and our people. I invited him to come to the church and conduct a week of special meetings.

David replied that he was booked up for the next year and a half. My heart sank because I didn't think I could last that long. Not long after this, I received a letter from David saying that he had had a cancellation and could come to our church in a few weeks. I happily booked him, and we started praying even more earnestly.

Just before David came for the special meetings, I said to my wife, "If God does not fill me with the Holy Spirit, I'm going to quit the ministry, go back to Canada, and get a job digging ditches. At least I will have some holes to show for what I do."

When David came for the eight days of special meetings, we had a time of prayer each weekday morning, and a time of prayer after each evening meeting for anyone who wanted to seek God for the baptism of the Holy Spirit. David consistently focused people on Jesus, and urged them to come to Jesus and drink, according to John 7:37-39:

> *Jesus stood [in the temple] and cried out, saying, "If anyone thirsts, let him come to Me and drink. He who believes in Me, as the Scripture has said, out of his heart will flow rivers of living water." But this He spoke concerning the Spirit, whom those believing in Him would receive.*

God Started to Pour Out His Spirit

In the first few days, some people were filled with the Holy Spirit and beautifully revived in their faith. But I was still dry and empty, and getting more and more desperate. During the prayer time on Wednesday morning, I could not stand it any longer. I left the prayer meeting and went into another room, knelt down with my elbows on a coffee table, and just stared at the floor. After a while, I felt an arm around my shoulders; it was David, kneeling beside me. God had given him a message for me. He had looked around the prayer room and saw that I was gone, so he went looking for me.

David said to me, "John, you have said to God, 'If You do not fill me with the Holy Spirit, I am going to quit the ministry.' You have no right saying that. If God has called you into the ministry, you have no right to quit until He tells you to quit. You are trying to blackmail God into doing for you what you want. He refuses to be treated that way. You owe it to Him to love Him and serve Him the rest of your life, just for dying for you and saving you, even if He does not do anything more for you." I began to protest, but David just said, "I'm not going to argue with you. God has spoken." And he got up and left.

I was completely taken aback. I went to my wife, Reta, and asked her if she had told David what I had said to her about me quitting the ministry. She said that she had not told him.

I had never before been spoken to like that, but I knew it was God. I was perplexed, but I knew I had to obey.

God Began to Fill Me

At the next meeting, in obedience, I began to love Jesus and worship Him. I took hymns that I had sung hundreds of times before, and now sang them with all the meaning and love and adoration I could pour out. During the next day or two, I opened up like a flower. The more I poured out love and worship to God, the more He poured out His Spirit on me. By the end of the week, I knew I had been quietly but greatly filled with the astounding Promise of the Father. He had filled me with the love and the joy of His Holy Spirit, and had revived me!

It is important to realize that, while some people have a dramatic experience and are filled instantly with God's Spirit, God has many ways of filling people. In my case, I was filled slowly and gradually. But God's ways are always right. Reta and I both expected to speak in tongues right away, but God gave us this gift about two years later, after we were back in Canada. Speaking in tongues is not the sole evidence of the baptism of the Holy Spirit. Any of the gifts of the Spirit are evidences of the Spirit, and He gives them as *He* wills (1 Corinthians 12:4-11; Romans 12:3-8).

When God filled me in Bombay, I had a new love for Jesus, for my wife and children, for the church people, and for the unsaved people around me. This God-love beyond human love, given by the Holy Spirit, began to grow and grow within me. The week after the special meetings, during my daily prayer time with God, I noticed that my love for the Lord was flowing as never before. And the Word of God was opening up to me and becoming much more alive. Before this, I had struggled all week to think about a subject for my sermon. Now, I had more things to preach than I knew what to do with. What a difference!

God Revived His People

Here is an incident I remember quite vividly: after the special meetings were over, we continued having the midweek prayer meetings. At one of these meetings, several of us felt God reveal to us that the head deacon was key to the revival continuing in the church. He had been giving me some trouble for quite a while, so we began to pray daily that God would fill him.

A few weeks later, as I was shaking hands with the people as they left the Sunday morning service, I saw this man next in line. Suddenly, I was filled with the love of God greater than ever before. As I shook his hand, I looked into his eyes and said, "God bless you, brother." A great wave of God's love flowed out of my eyes, out of my voice, and out of my hands. I was totally surprised at this, and he was startled and didn't know what to do. Within two or three weeks, he also was filled with the Spirit and revived.

The Holy Spirit continued to work in the congregation. More and more people were filled with the Spirit and revived. Others realized that they needed to receive Christ and be born again. More unbelievers were coming and getting saved. People from other congregations were coming to be filled with the Holy Spirit, and then returning to their churches with new life. When my year of pastoring the church was up, the deacons were unanimous in asking me to continue.

God Established the Church

We were far from perfect, but we had been revived and transformed. Jesus was still correcting and cleansing us, and also growing and maturing us.

The work of the Holy Spirit continued long after we left. Eventually the church was pastored by Indian pastors, not missionaries. Some of these Indian pastors began to train their young people and send them out to start new churches in the suburbs of this great city. Today, more than three hundred churches have been planted and the work is continuing.

HEARING GOD SPEAK TO US PERSONALLY

Since being filled with the Holy Spirit, I have found that I am more sensitive to recognize His voice. God speaks to us and guides us in many different ways, although I am sure we often fail to recognize that His voice is speaking in our hearts.

Throughout this book, I have shared with you times when God spoke to me very strongly and clearly through His Spirit. Here is one more.

One time, I was attending a conference on revival. One of the speakers quoted Ezekiel 22:30–31, where God says,

> *So I sought for a man among them who would make a wall, and stand in the gap [breach] before Me on behalf of the land, that I should not destroy it; but I found no one. Therefore I have poured out My indignation on them; I have consumed them with the fire of My wrath.*

Ezekiel gave this prophecy at a time when God's people had, for several centuries, turned to worshipping idols rather than God. Because of this idolatry, God had sent the nation of Babylon to besiege and capture the walled city of Jerusalem. The Babylonians had breached the wall, plundered the city, and taken many captives, including Ezekiel. This is when God said, *"I sought for a man among them."*

As I thought about it, I was startled that God would seek just one man to stand in the gap for the whole city and nation to save them. Then I heard, in my spirit, God say strongly and clearly, "I want you to be such a man to stand in the gap for My church."

Now, throughout the Old Testament, the nation of Israel and the city of Jerusalem are a prophetic picture of the New Testament church. So God was taking a verse from the Old Testament and applying it to our situation today.

I immediately began to say, "Lord, I don't know how to do that. I am weak and foolish, and a nothing and a nobody." Then

He said to me, "Those are the kind of people I usually choose" (see 1 Corinthians 1:26-29).

I knew that I had to obey, and that this was one of the main assignments for my life: to intercede for a great outpouring of the Holy Spirit to revive His whole church.

Since then, from time to time, God has given me more than a dozen short words of prophecy, to encourage me to continue to stand in the gap and not give up. These prophesies have come through different people, some who didn't even know me, and at different times. They said either one of two things: "You will live long enough to see the greatest passion of your heart" or "You are a Simeon (see Luke 2:25–35); you are going to see with your eyes what you have been longing for."

I'm eighty-two years old as of the publishing of this book— so the great outpouring of the Holy Spirit must be close!

I strongly urge you to join me in making this great outpouring of God's Holy Spirit one of the main requests in our times of prayer and intercession. God is looking for intercessors (Isaiah 59:16).

CHAPTER ELEVEN

THE BEST IS YET TO COME

I s the measure of the fullness of the Holy Spirit we presently experience all that we are going to get? Or is there a greater measure of the fullness and power of the Holy Spirit coming to God's church in the future? Is there reason to expect, and pray for, another powerful outpouring of the Holy Spirit before Jesus returns for His church?

Yes, I do believe that God will give a great outpouring of His Holy Spirit across the whole world before Jesus returns. And I see some scriptures that indicate this. I want to share these with you, and share my joyful and passionate expectation of this great outpouring.

A CLOSER LOOK AT JOEL'S PROPHECY

We have already looked at Joel's prophecy of the outpouring of the Holy Spirit. Let's take another look at the situation and the conditions in the nation of Israel in Joel's time. This will provide a context for the astounding promise God gave in Joel 2:28-32.

The Context

As we have seen, at the time of Joel's prophecy, God's people were experiencing a terrible drought which produced crop failure and severe famine. They also had been invaded by a plague of locusts. This had occurred because they were not obeying Him and had fallen into idolatry.

Many years before, God appeared to King Solomon and told him that God is the One who sends drought, famine, locusts, and plagues. He does this when His people have turned away from Him, because He is trying to draw them back to Himself (2 Chronicles 6:24-31). God promises that if His people will humble themselves, pray and seek His face, and repent of their wicked ways, He will hear from heaven, forgive their sin, and heal their land (2 Chronicles 7:13-14). This warning and promise applied to God's people in the days of the prophet Joel.

So God raised up the prophet Joel, who cried out to the Israelites to:

- wake up, weep, lament, mourn, and be ashamed;
- consecrate a fast and call a sacred meeting of the people to cry out to the Lord;
- raise an alarm to alert the people of coming judgment;
- turn to the Lord wholeheartedly, with fasting, weeping, and mourning;
- tear their hearts, not their clothes, to show true repentance; and
- return to God, Who is full of grace and mercy, not easily angered, and very kind (see Joel 1:5–2:17).

God Responds to Repentance and Intercession

As God promised Solomon, so God promised His people through Joel:

> *Then the* LORD *will be zealous for His land, and pity His people. The* LORD *will answer and say to His people, "Behold, I will send you grain and new wine and [olive] oil" ...Be glad then, you children of Zion, and rejoice in the* LORD *your God; for He has given you the former rain faithfully, and He will cause the rain to come down for you—the former rain, and the latter rain in the first month. The threshing floors shall be full of wheat, and the vats shall overflow with new wine and [olive] oil.*
>
> —Joel 2:18-19, 23-24

A Double Downpour

In Israel, in the normal annual weather cycle, the "former rain" came in the fall, and was fairly heavy. It loosened the ground, allowing the farmers to plow their fields and plant their crops. Throughout the winter, there were occasional rain showers. Then in the spring, the "latter rains" came. These rains were heavier, causing the grain to quickly come to a head and ripen, and produce a good harvest.

But here in Joel 2:23, God says something highly unusual and very important. He promises to give the "former rain" and the "latter rain" in the same month, causing the threshing floors to be full, and the vats of wine and oil to overflow. God promised a "double downpour," with an abundant crop as a result—when His people repent and intercede!

Then God says,

> *And it shall come to pass afterward that I will pour out
> My Spirit on all flesh [peoples]… before the coming of
> the great and awesome day of the LORD.*
>
> —Joel 2:28, 31

I think it is significant that in Joel 2:23–24, God mentioned the "former rain" and "latter rain" coming together as a double downpour, just before He gave the prophecy of the later worldwide outpouring of His Holy Spirit, His astounding promise. Could this be an indication that He will give a double downpour of His Holy Spirit in the last days, to prepare His church for Christ's return?

Applied to the Church Today

The kingdom of Israel, God's *earthly* chosen people, is a prophetic picture and type of His church, God's *spiritually* chosen people. We are encouraged to learn from what Israel experienced in Joel's day.

> *For whatever things were written before were written
> for our learning, that we through the patience and comfort of the [Old Testament] Scriptures might have hope.*
>
> —Romans 15:4 (emphasis added)

*Now all these things happened to them [the Israelites]
as examples, and they were written for our admonition, upon whom the ends of the ages have come.*
—1 Corinthians 10:11 (emphasis added);
see also verses 6–10

Therefore, the condition of Israel's drought and famine, what God urged them to do and what God promised to do for them if they obeyed, can be applied to Jesus' church today.

This is especially the case with the church in North America and Europe, in its present spiritual condition. Recently, I read that the annual growth rate of the church in the Western world is negligible, while the growth rate of much of the church in the rest of the world is quite healthy. From what I can see, the Western church is in a spiritual drought and experiencing a tragic crop failure, with few lost souls receiving Jesus and being born again—because of our many sins and subtle idolatries.

Does this make your heart cry out to God for revival and a great harvest of lost souls? We greatly need a double downpour of the Holy Spirit to produce this harvest—for His pleasure and glory!

Jesus Says, "Be zealous and repent"

Let us *not* be like the church of the Laodiceans in Revelation 3:14–20, which considered itself rich, increased with goods, and in need of nothing, but they didn't know they were lukewarm, wretched, miserable, poor, blind, and naked. Jesus called them to be *zealous* and *repent*.

The promise God made to King Solomon, which applied to the people in Joel's time, also applies to us today:

When I shut up heaven and there is no rain, or command the locusts to devour the land, or send pestilence [plague] among My people, if My people who are called by My name will humble *themselves, and pray and seek My face [closeness, intimacy], and turn [repent] from their wicked ways, then I will hear from heaven, and will forgive their sin and heal their land.*
—2 Chronicles 7:13-14 (emphasis added)

Notice that God promises His blessings—to hear our prayers, forgive our sins, and heal our land—but there are actions we must take. We must first humble ourselves, pray and seek closeness and intimacy with God, then repent, turning away from our sins, including the many ways we incline our lives to worldly pleasures and pursuits rather than to God.

Let us hear in *our* spirits what God said through Joel to the people of his day: "Wake up! Mourn, weep, cry out to the Lord, and turn to the Lord with all your heart." God will be gracious and merciful. He will give us the former rain and the latter rain in the same month. A great harvest of lost souls will receive Jesus, become born again, and be filled to overflowing with the Holy Spirit, for His glory and pleasure.

Ask the Lord for the Rain, and Wait Patiently

Ask the Lord *for rain in the time of the latter rain. The* Lord *will make flashing clouds; He will give them showers of rain, grass in the field for everyone.*
—Zechariah 10:1 (emphasis added)

Ask and then be patient, waiting in faith for God to answer and fulfill His promise to us, in *His* way and in *His* time. God wants us to keep asking until He does what He has promised. Keep your request before His throne of grace!

Therefore be patient, brethren, until the coming of the Lord. See how the farmer waits for the precious fruit of the earth, waiting patiently for it until it receives the early [former] and latter rain. You also be patient. Establish [encourage and strengthen] your hearts, for the coming of the Lord is at hand [near].

—James 5:7–8

ANOTHER LOOK AT THE DAY OF PENTECOST

When the Lord filled the 120 disciples with His Holy Spirit, the sound of a mighty rushing wind caused a great crowd from Jerusalem to gather together. Many of these people were from different countries, coming to celebrate the Feast of Pentecost, the Feast of Harvest. When they heard these disciples glorifying God in their various native languages, they did not understand what was happening (Acts 2:5–13). So Peter explained that

this is what was spoken by the prophet Joel: "And it shall come to pass in the last days, says God, that I will pour out of My Spirit on all flesh; your sons and your daughters shall prophesy, your young men shall see visions, your old men shall dream dreams. And on My menservants and on My maidservants I will pour out My Spirit in those days; and they shall prophesy...

before *the coming of the great and awesome [notable]
day of the LORD."*
—Acts 2:16-18, 20 (emphasis added)

What Time Is It?

Clearly, Peter was filled with the Holy Spirit when he quoted the prophecy from Joel. The Holy Spirit said through Peter that God would pour out His Spirit on all flesh "in the last days." The timeframe is quite specific.

But when God first spoke the prophecy through Joel, He said that He would pour His Spirit on all flesh "afterward" (Joel 2:28). Here, the timeframe is indefinite.

Did the Holy Spirit make a mistake when He spoke through Peter? Did the Holy Spirit misquote Joel when Peter said, *"And it shall come to pass in the last days"?* No way! The Holy Spirit cannot make errors! God is giving us an insight into the period of history when the last great outpouring of the Spirit will happen.

"It shall come to pass in the last days"

After Jesus' ascension into heaven, angels appeared to His disciples and told them, *"This same Jesus, who was taken up from you into heaven, will so come in like manner as you saw Him go into heaven"* (Acts 1:11). Then, on the day of Pentecost, the Holy Spirit was poured out on the disciples in fulfillment of Joel's prophecy. So I am sure the disciples were expecting Jesus to return—His second coming—in their lifetime. They must have thought they were in "the last days" before His return. And rightfully so, for they had heard the angels' words and shortly afterward experienced the fulfillment of Joel's prophecy.

But if you examine Joel's prophecy, you will see that there were some things that were *not yet* fulfilled when God poured out His Spirit in the book of Acts. He has yet to pour out His Spirit on *all* peoples (Joel 2:28). The wonders in the heavens and in the earth—blood and fire and pillars of smoke, the sun darkened, and the moon turned into blood—have *yet* to happen (Joel 2:30-31). And Jesus has not yet returned, even though generation after generation of Christians since the first disciples have believed—to this point, wrongly—that they were living in the last days and that Jesus would return in their lifetime.

I believe God's design is that every generation of Christians should be expecting and longing for Christ's return in their lifetime. Based on this, I believe that "the last days" must mean the entire church age—from Jesus' ascension until His return—so that "afterward" and "the last days" includes today.

So was the outpouring of the Holy Spirit described in Acts 2 and the succeeding chapters the complete and final fulfillment of Joel's prophecy? If the day of Pentecost was the beginning of "afterward" or "the last days," then perhaps the outpouring of the Holy Spirit on that day was just the beginning of God's astounding promise through Joel as reiterated by Peter. Without wanting to minimize one little bit what the early church experienced, I believe it was *not the total fulfillment* of Joel's prophecy, but merely a wonderful and astounding beginning. It was a great foretaste of that which is to come. It was the "former rain" that got the crop started.

There have been many revivals throughout church history since the initial outpouring. I am thankful for them. However, these were like occasional showers during the winter. Now it is very close to two thousand years after the initial outpouring in Acts 2. I believe we are seeing many of the terrible things that

Scripture says would happen in the last days before Christ's return. And I see quite a few signs of God preparing for a "latter rain," the last great outpouring of His Holy Spirit. This rain will be heavy, to prepare for the great harvest of lost souls and to prepare His Bride, the church, for the great wedding feast!

THE HIGHEST PRIORITY

I have shared with you how God has called me to intercede for a great outpouring of the Holy Spirit to revive His whole church. God has helped me to gradually understand and grow in this assignment. However, God also has had to caution me to keep that assignment in perspective.

It happened when I was in a large convention. The Holy Spirit had said to the leader that he was to ask for a time of complete silence. I admired the man for having the courage to obey. So the whole audience was in silence for quite some time. Having that many charismatic Christians remain silent for such a long period of time was a miracle in itself!

Quite a while passed. I was just staring at the floor when I heard the Lord Jesus call my name and say, "John, what is the greatest passion of your heart?"

I was quick to answer Him, saying, "It is for a great outpouring of Your Holy Spirit that will produce a great revival in Your church and give a great harvest of lost souls coming to You."

Then Jesus said to me, "It's *not Me* anymore, is it?"

I could somehow hear and feel His great disappointment, sadness, and loneliness. Instantly I understood what He meant. My passion for a great outpouring of the Holy Spirit had been so great that in my daily devotional times I had gotten right down to business interceding for this. This had *crowded out* my time of love, worship, adoration, and gratitude with Jesus. No longer was I spending time just loving, worshipping, praising, and listening to Him.

I began to sob deeply. But I had to sob silently, so as not to disturb the silence in the room! When I had finished sobbing, Jesus said to me lovingly and tenderly, "*Either* the work of the Lord *or* the Lord of the work will come first. You must choose."

This has been a profound lesson in my life, to keep proper priorities and maintain a Christ-centered balance. In some ways, I am now more burdened than ever before for the outpouring of the Spirit to revive the church. However, Jesus Himself is the greatest passion, the burning love, of my heart.

So God will speak to us by His Spirit to lead us into ministry. But that must never overshadow our love-relationship with God, Jesus, and the Holy Spirit.

A SHORT SUMMARY

I want to reiterate the main themes of this book, as simply and clearly as I can, so that you will see God's master plan.

When God lovingly created Adam, as His own precious child, He filled Adam's spirit with His own Spirit. But when Adam sinned, God's Holy Spirit left him, and Adam's spirit died and was left empty. This condition was passed on from Adam to all the rest of us, God's precious, precious family.

But God still greatly loved us all, and intensely desired us all to be united with Him again. So God prophesied that He would send a Savior to reconcile us back to Himself. God also prophesied that He would make a new covenant with us and put His Spirit back into us.

In fulfillment of the first prophecy, God came to us as a human, Jesus, to die and atone for the sins of the whole human race. Through Jesus' crucifixion and resurrection we can receive total forgiveness and eternal life. With our sins totally forgiven and blotted out, God's Holy Spirit can come into us and fill us.

God prophesied through Joel that there will be a great outpouring of His Spirit upon all peoples. The outpouring on the day of Pentecost was the great beginning, but not the final fulfillment of Joel's prophecy. God said that the great worldwide outpouring would be in "the last days," before the return of Christ. I believe this is near, and we should humble ourselves, pray, seek His face, repent, and expect it.

The fullness and power of God's Holy Spirit in us is God's astounding promise for us all!

"FILLED WITH ALL THE FULLNESS OF GOD"

The apostle Paul prayed

> that Christ may dwell in your hearts through faith; that you, being rooted and grounded in love, may be able to comprehend with all the saints [believers] what is the width and length and depth and height—to know [experience] the love of Christ which passes [surpasses] knowledge; that you may be filled with all the fullness of God.
> —Ephesians 3:17-19 (emphasis added)

This is what the astounding promise is all about. This is what God has for His precious Bride, His last-days church. This is my prayer for myself, and my prayer for you and for the worldwide body of Christ. Ask God to fill you with *all His fullness*. It is His astounding promise and gift for us *all!*

But don't stop there! Paul told the believers in the city of Ephesus to be filled with the Spirit, even though they had already been baptized in the Holy Spirit (Ephesians 5:18). In the Greek text, the verb "be filled" is a present/progressive tense which means to be filled and keep on being filled. Let's go on continually with Jesus, receiving more and more of His Spirit. Thirst for more, come to Jesus daily, and drink deeply. He who drinks in faith, out of his heart will flow *rivers* of living water (John 7:37-38).

HOW TO RECEIVE AND BE FILLED WITH THE HOLY SPIRIT

The baptism of the Spirit is a prophecy, a promise, a command, and a gift, but it is *not* an option! We must act, by opening ourselves and receiving it. Here's how.

1. Obey Jesus' command. He told the disciples *"to wait for the Promise of the Father,"* the baptism of the Holy Spirit, until they were endued with power from heaven (Acts 1:4-5).
2. Ask, believing in God's promise. Jesus promised that if we ask, and keep on asking, it will be given. If we seek, and keep seeking, we will find. If we knock, and keep on knocking, it will be opened to us. For *everyone* who asks will receive (Luke 11:9-13). Many experience the baptism in the Holy Spirit as soon as they ask, and others experience it later on. God has to prepare some of us until we are ready. God has His own perfect time for each of us!
3. Receive, by faith, and thank Him in advance. "Please give" is the language of asking, while "Thank You" is the language of receiving. Claim this gift and thank Him for it in advance,

because it is God's promise and He cannot break His astounding promise. It is His free gift, by His grace. None of us can ever deserve it, work for it, or earn it (Galatians 3:14).

4. Wait, expecting God to give you the gift of His Spirit, in His own way, and in His own time. God is sure to give. He will never break His promises! (1 Thessalonians 5:24)

5. Keep on being filled. Jesus said, *"If anyone thirsts, let him come to Me and drink [and keep drinking]... out of his heart will flow rivers of living water"* (John 7:37–38).

DEAR READER

Have you *received* (not just passively believed in) the crucified and resurrected Jesus Christ as your Savior and Lord? He died on that cross, paid for all your sin, and offers you the gift of forgiveness and eternal life. But you must *receive* Him (an action) and the free gift He offers you.

> *But as many as* received *Him [Jesus], to them He gave the right to become children of God, to those who believe in His name.*
>
> —John 1:12 (emphasis added)

Say it out loud to Him. This is important! God promises

> *that if you confess with your mouth the Lord Jesus and believe in your heart that God has raised Him from the dead, you will be saved. For with the heart one believes unto righteousness, and with the mouth confession is made unto salvation.*
>
> —Romans 10:9-10

Behold, He stands at the door of your heart and knocks. He calls out to you, inviting you to open the door and verbally invite Him in as your Savior and Lord. He is saying,

> *If anyone hears My voice and opens the door,* I will come in *to him and dine [feast] with him, and he with Me.*
> —Revelation 3:20 (emphasis added)

Turn to Him in repentance and say, "Jesus, I invite You to come in. I *receive* You and Your salvation into my heart and life. I want to follow You, love You, and serve You. Put Your Spirit *into* my spirit and begin, by Your power, to make me a new creation."

If you have already received Him and have been born again, have you *received* His astounding promise of the baptism, fullness, and power of His Holy Spirit? Have you come to Him, given yourself completely to Him, and by faith *received all* that He has for you?

Jesus said,

> *If anyone thirsts, let him come to Me and drink. He who believes in Me, as the Scripture has said, out of his heart will flow* rivers of living water.
> —John 7:37-38 (emphasis added)

God's Spirit is the *only* source of the power to live and love God's way. Have you *received* Him?

ALSO BY JOHN G. HUTCHINSON

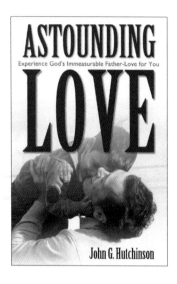

*Astounding Love: Experience God's
Immeasurable Father-Love for You*

ISBN: 9781770691414

Do you think of God as being somewhat strict and harsh or cold
and distant? Do you feel that He mostly wants to find fault and
condemn? *Astounding Love* reveals God's great love and goodness, and His burning desire for a close, loving relationship with
us all. If you want to discover—and experience—God's beautiful,
true, loving character, this book is for you. And it could also be a
great gift for someone you know who needs this kind of love!

Available through Amazon, Chapters/Indigo,
astoundingfatherlove.com and wherever
fine Christian books are sold.

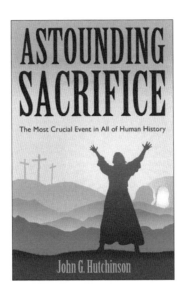

Astounding Sacrifice: The Most Crucial
Event in All of Human History

ISBN: 9781770696532

Was Jesus' crucifixion just a tragic untimely end to a wonderful life? Why did God allow this to happen? What is the whole story? Author John Hutchinson has woven together, into one harmonious narrative, every detail of Jesus' crucifixion, resurrection, and ascension from the four Gospels, to give a more complete picture and a richer insight into the most crucial event in all of human history. *Astounding Sacrifice* describes the immense price that God and Jesus willingly paid to bring us back into a love relationship with Him for eternity.

Available through Amazon, Chapters/Indigo,
astoundingfatherlove.com and wherever
fine Christian books are sold.